A U.S. FOREIGN POLICY FOR ASIA

The 1980s and Beyond

RAMON H. MYERS
editor

HOOVER INSTITUTION PRESS
Stanford University | Stanford, California

The Hoover Institution on War, Revolution and Peace, founded at Stanford University in 1919 by the late President Herbert Hoover, is an interdisciplinary research center for advanced study on domestic and international affairs in the twentieth century. The views expressed in its publications are entirely those of the authors and do not necessarily reflect the views of the staff, officers, or Board of Overseers of the Hoover Institution.

Hoover Press Publication 271

© 1982 by the Board of Trustees of the
  Leland Stanford Junior University
All rights reserved
International Standard Book Number: 0-8179-7712-0
Library of Congress Catalog Card Number: 81-84642
Printed in the United States of America

DS
33.4
U6
U54
1982

WITHDRAWN

A U.S. FOREIGN POLICY FOR ASIA

HOOVER INTERNATIONAL STUDIES
Richard F. Staar, director

The Panama Canal Controversy
Paul B. Ryan

The Imperialist Revolutionaries
Hugh Seton-Watson

South Africa: War, Revolution, or Peace?
L.H. Gann and Peter Duignan

Two Chinese States
Ramon H. Myers, editor

The Clouded Lens: Persian Gulf Security, second ed.
James H. Noyes

Soviet Strategy for Nuclear War
Joseph D. Douglass, Jr., and Amoretta M. Hoeber

Science, Technology and China's Drive for Moderation
Richard P. Suttmeier

The End of the Tito Era
Slobodan Stanković

Waiting for a "Pearl Harbor": Japan Debates Defense
Tetsuya Kataoka

Afghanistan: The Soviet Invasion in Perspective
Anthony Arnold

Communist Powers and Sub-Saharan Africa
Thomas H. Henriksen, editor

The United States and the Republic of Korea
Claude A. Buss

Communism in Central America and the Caribbean
Robert Wesson, editor

Ideology of a Superpower
R. Judson Mitchell

The ASEAN States and Regional Security
Sheldon W. Simon

A U.S. Foreign Policy for Asia
Ramon H. Myers, editor

To my mother—in the hope
her grandchildren will live in a world of peace

CONTENTS

Foreword   ix

Introduction   xi
    Ramon H. Myers

1 | U.S. Foreign Policy for Asia   1
    Ray S. Cline

2 | U.S. Foreign Policy in the 1980s: South and Southwest Asia   17
    Walter K. Andersen

3 | U.S. Policy in Asia: The India Factor   38
    Leo E. Rose

4 | Toward a U.S. Security Policy in Southeast Asia: A Maritime Emphasis   60
    Sheldon W. Simon

5 | Japan and Northeast Asia   74
    Donald C. Hellmann

6 | The U.S. Position in Asia and the Pacific: The Relevance of Australia and New Zealand   89
    Henry S. Albinski

7 | The U.S. Role in East and Southeast Asia   114
    Franklin B. Weinstein

Contributors   141

Index   143

Foreword

The collection of papers in this volume originates from a conference organized by Ramon H. Myers, curator-scholar and senior fellow of the Hoover Institution, and convened at the Hoover Institution, Stanford University in April 1981. There are several features about this volume that deserve special comment.

First, the writers of these essays display a broad range of expertise. All salient areas of Asia today are examined in an informative and insightful way for policymakers in Washington. These scholars have traveled in the areas of Asia about which they write, and several have been involved in important government agencies or departments responsible for making foreign policy. Each has closely followed and studied the contemporary events of that Asian subregion of his expertise. Their account of the current political difficulties and security problems facing the major Asian countries is extremely valuable and presented from the perspective of the dilemmas perceived by those governments in Asia at this time.

Second, this volume strikes a remarkable balance between the complex issues of Asian military security, the economic problems Asian countries face, and the diplomatic difficulties between Asian states with border problems, an achievement rare in geopolitical studies of this kind.

As a new Republican administration tries to formulate an American foreign policy while solving the serious problems at home, the debate over the appropriate direction of America's foreign policy in the world gradually heats up. What is urgently needed at this critical time are international perspectives that are geopolitical and yet country-specific while clearly presenting an agenda of priority issues that deserve a policy. This volume certainly does that while advancing a series of recommendations that are well within America's capability to act.

Many will find the essays in this volume provocative and controversial. It hits hard at certain sacrosanct positions long favored amongst Asian foreign policy analysts. While doing so, it suggests new directions for diplomacy that policymakers will ignore at their peril.

By recommending that Asia's strategic importance be considered equal to that of Europe, by advancing a new framework to re-examine the Afghanistan and Cambodian conflicts, by elevating the strategic importance of India to that of China, and by stressing that America strive to improve its bilateral relations with the Asian Pacific-basin countries, this volume advances a new foreign policy design for Asia that policymakers and experts should find informative and useful.

RICHARD F. STAAR

Director of International Studies
Hoover Institution

INTRODUCTION

Since the 1970s, U.S. foreign policy has failed to check the dynamic imperialism of the Soviet Union, and conflicts in various parts of the world have threatened the balance of power between these two superpowers and world peace itself. This failure in U.S. foreign policy is evident in Asia.

Because of the current wars raging in Cambodia and Afghanistan, Soviet influence has expanded in the Indochina peninsula and in Afghanistan. Ruled by Marxist-Leninist parties, three socialist states have been solidly established on the Asian subcontinent in the past four decades, and their very existence has aggravated tensions between various countries: North and South Korea; China and the Soviet Union; China and Vietnam; Vietnam and Thailand. Other tension points also exist between the Soviet Union and Japan and between India and Pakistan, yet U.S. foreign policy has always focused on NATO and the security of Western Europe since World War II. In the past few years, that policy has been modified to focus on the People's Republic of China as a power to help check the Soviet Union and to rearm Japan as a new power to help maintain the security of the Pacific.

This collection of essays raises serious questions about the effectiveness of current U.S. foreign policy in Asia. With assessments of the present state of political affairs in Asia and the undesirable consequences that can flow from such a policy, these seven chapters argue that U.S. national interests and the peace and security of Asia would be better served by a different posture abroad. The new foreign policy proposed in the following pages focuses on the economic and political value of those key noncommunist nations encircling eastern and southern Asia (here referred to as the Asian Pacific-basin nations) and also India.

America needs a foreign policy that can counter Soviet expansionism, advanced by the two wars now raging in Asia, and cool tensions among various states. The current U.S. policy of tilting toward China and rearming Japan runs the grave risk of perpetuating current conflicts and aggravating existing international tensions. Why? Because most Asian states are beset by extraordinary difficulties and have extremely poor options for guaranteeing their national security while still maintaining domestic political stability. In the face of these complex conditions, we perceive the limits of American power and the need for a new American policy in Asia.

The new foreign policy argued in this volume aims to restore and maintain a balance of power between states in the key geopolitical regions of Asia. This policy must be built upon existing strengths, not on political weakness and uncertainty. Such a policy, moreover, must have the support of this country's public opinion. Let us briefly consider these matters in greater detail.

Asia in the Early 1980s

We should first be clear about present dangers and predicaments surrounding Asia's conflicts and tension points in the early 1980s. We can then understand the delicate security concerns of pivotal Asian states and see how American policy so far has failed to take these concerns into account.

Southwest Asia

In the past decade, the center of crisis in Asia has shifted from the east and southeast to the southwest. This "arc of crisis," extending from Turkey to India, denotes a region where stable regimes that were once friendly to the West and particularly to the United States have collapsed and have been replaced by unstable governments hostile to the United States. Afghanistan even fell into the sphere of Soviet influence, although its influence only embraces Kabul and a few large cities, not the countryside. Led by Muslim fundamentalists, Iran now appears to be threatened by civil war.

To restore the balance of power in this region requires either Soviet willingness to withdraw from Afghanistan, leaving that country in the hands of a politically neutral leadership or of a new military capability created to offset possible Soviet aggression. The United States faces serious difficulties in achieving either goal. Our allies do not perceive the recent shift of balance of power as unfavorable to the West as does the United States. Our European allies view the Afghan crisis as isolated from the European scene and a north-south issue (between the wealthy, industrial countries of the north and the poorer nations of the south), so they have opted for an international conference with Soviet participation to resolve the Afghan problem; India also favors this approach to a resolution. Negotiations, however, have broken down over the inclusion of a representative of the Babrak Karmal regime.

U.S. leaders who make foreign policy have proposed strengthening Pakistan's economic foundations and military security and increasing the American naval presence near the Persian Gulf and in the Indian Ocean. This strategy is beset with twin difficulties: the national security choices of both Pakistan and India are extremely poor. Unless the United States skillfully deals with these two issues, its strategy of bolstering Pakistan as a counterweight for a Soviet-supported regime in Afghanistan will founder.

Both Pakistan's and India's security concerns must be viewed within the context of their historical political and military rivalry. The two countries have waged three wars against each other since 1947, chiefly over the state of Kashmir; each views the other with extreme distrust and fear. Aside from a history of conflict, both countries are poor and have unstable political systems. Pakistan contains numerous ethnic groups of different Islamic faiths. Pakistan, moreover, does not trust the Soviet Union; its Islamic allies are distant and weak. Although China might supply arms to Pakistan, it cannot be depended upon if Pakistan goes to war with India or the Soviet Union. Pakistan's leaders feel their country is surrounded by enemies. These same leaders also have a weak hold over the country, and, although the economy is currently sound, large transfers of aid and sophisticated weaponry might destabilize it. The Pakistani government needs long-term assurances from Washington, which must relate to Pakistan's complex security concerns.

The political situation in India is also precarious. India, too, fears the Soviet involvement in Afghanistan, but it equally fears the emergence of a powerful Islamic republic on its doorstep. An expanded American military presence is not welcome in the region because that might elicit a counterresponse from the Soviet Union. Also, India must contend with awesome domestic problems and a population of ethnic and cultural diversity that makes democratic governance a political nightmare.

U.S. policy ought to be extremely cautious in this region and constantly take into account the Pakistani-Indian rivalry and their complex security concerns. A failure to do that might spell disaster; war between the two nations or political turmoil in Pakistan would open the door to chaos.

Southeast Asia

A few years ago Laos became a client of Vietnam, but so far Vietnam has not been able to bring Cambodia into its orbit of rule. The Vietnam-backed Heng Samrin government in Phnom Penh has been unable to defeat the Khmer Rouge forces of Pol Pot to govern all of Cambodia, now called Democratic Kampuchea. Vietnam's effort to control Indochina has been vigorously opposed by China, which prefers that Indochina consist of three separate states rather than one under Vietnamese hegemony. China has supported the Khmer Rouge with military aid and through its foreign policy of mobilizing international support for the Cambodian government of the Khmer Rouge.

The United States has endorsed the Chinese position, and although refusing to support the Khmer Rouge directly, it has expressed public disapproval of the Heng Samrin regime and Vietnam's military action in Cambodia. The Association for Southeast Asian Nations (ASEAN), meanwhile, has pursued an ambiguous foreign policy toward Indochina, avoiding any expression of support for the positions of Hanoi or Beijing. The ASEAN states also have united behind Thailand and encouraged international public opinion to pressure Vietnam to withdraw its forces from Cambodia.

An ailing economy, the exodus of skilled labor, and conflict with China have compelled Vietnam to turn to the Soviet Union for military and economic aid. As Vietnam increasingly depends upon Moscow, Soviet influence in Indochina has greatly increased: thousands of advisers have poured into the region, Soviet planes have used Vietnamese airfields, and the Soviet Navy has taken advantage of the large ports built by the United States.

The Indochina conflict has all the qualities of a serious clan feud whereby both parties depend upon outsiders for support, but are determined to struggle until the bitter end. When the Khmer Rouge forces weaken, China increases its aid. Refugees then pour into Thailand to receive aid. China breaks off negotiations with Hanoi over the border problem and threatens to teach Vietnam a lesson. In turn, Vietnam requests more economic and military aid from the Soviet Union to prop up its failing economy and support the Heng Samrin regime of Kampuchea. Hanoi also demands that Thailand stop aid to the Cambodian refugees, charging that too much aid is routed to the Khmer Rouge. The Cambodian conflict grinds on, always threatening to spill over into China or Thailand.

The ASEAN states have been searching without success for a formula to resolve this conflict. They have doubled their military expenditures between 1975 and 1980, and they frequently have held joint military maneuvers. These states, however, are not likely to risk all-out war if Vietnam takes greater military action to punish Thailand. Meanwhile, they are trying to shoulder a heavy military burden, which their fragile economies cannot support without incurring inflation and domestic unrest. Although the leaders are determined, the politically and economically weak governments of ASEAN countries are often under attack by critics at home.

How, then, will it be possible to overcome the impasse in Indochina, resolve the military conflict, and reduce Soviet military presence in the region? By supporting the current Chinese foreign policy, the United States runs a grave risk of increasing the military burden for its ASEAN allies and having the Cambodian conflict extend into Thailand. America's current Southeast Asia policy continues to encourage a protracted war in Indochina in the hope it will weaken Vietnamese resolve and create an independent regime in Kampuchea. So far, that has not happened, and the Soviet influence in Indochina steadily grows.

East Asia

Like no other year since 1945, 1981 marked a turning point for Japan. In the past 30 years Japan became a world economic power without having to pay for its national security, which was guaranteed by the United States. Pacifism became deeply rooted in the Japanese psyche. Japan's polity, conservative in ideology, still was controlled by the Liberal Democratic Party, which could split at any time and produce a crisis of governance. Dependent upon exports and opposed to spending more for defense, the Japanese viewed the world with Panglossian optimism until 1972.

Thereafter, oil—its life blood—became enormously expensive. Exports, the mainstay of its economy, were resisted in those world markets that counted most: America and Western Europe. Its security was eroding as the United States kept insisting that Japan contribute more for its own security. Japan's neighbor to the north, the Soviet Union, began to appear more threatening by expanding naval power, building more ballistic missiles in Siberia, and stationing a battalion of troops on the contested four southernmost Kurile Islands. Then, in the spring of 1981, relations with the United States took a turn for the worse.

The Reagan administration overreacted to domestic economic pressures and demanded that Japan limit automobile exports to the United States. The Pentagon stridently insisted that Japan increase its spending for defense. Then came the fateful sinking of a Japanese freighter by an American submarine, and several American ships destroyed the fishing nets of Japanese trawlers. A former American ambassador to Japan disclosed that American nuclear warheads probably had found their way into Japan. Finally, the unfortunate wording of the joint communiqué by Prime Minister

Suzuki and President Reagan, after their first meeting, set off waves of anti-Americanism rarely seen in Japan.

As with so many other countries, Japan now must choose between guns or butter, and this choice comes at an awkward time. The government has already pledged to restructure the Japanese economy during the 1980s to reduce export dependency while also seeking to reduce oil imports by expanding nuclear power at home. These measures require fiscal fine tuning to keep a balanced budget. But America's leaders, projecting that proconsul toughness of the former occupation era, demand that the Japanese lower their tariffs, admit more American goods, and still spend more for defense.

The Japanese have become bitterly divided over what to do about their national security. Some view the recent Soviet military buildup in Siberia as a real threat to Japan, but others attribute it to the USSR's protection of its frontier with China. Opinions are also sharply divided about future Sino-Japanese relations, with a majority still worrying about the political stability of China. Japanese leaders are also sensitive to reactions from South Korea and Southeast Asia toward any sudden increase in military spending, fearing negative consequences for foreign trade.

Japan's current dilemmas are serious. Any political decision to spend more for defense must take account of strong domestic opposition. And the money for defense must be found, although the government has already committed itself to long-term projects for guaranteeing the restructuring and stability of the economy. Japan must ascertain how much it is really threatened from the north and if it is in its best interests to develop a strong alliance with China. These are some of the many problems that Japan's leaders now ponder and which American foreign policy must take into account.

The situation in China is hardly better. China's leaders are currently struggling to rebuild the Communist Party, modernize the economy, and restore the education and scientific establishments so severely damaged during those years of political turmoil euphemistically referred to as The Great Cultural Revolution. It is highly problematic whether China can maintain political stability as it tries to carry out these tasks.

China's dilemma is not simply that it is extremely poor and overpopulated. More serious, its people, particularly party cadres, are demoralized and skeptical about the superiority and workability of socialism. Dissent currently rages as various groups ranging from pro-Soviet to pro-Mao still clandestinely publish and distribute their political tracts despite confiscations and arrests. China's leaders, therefore, must now struggle to restore the legitimacy of the Communist Party. They must also stamp out dissent without resorting to widespread terror. On the economic front, they fight a difficult battle to dampen inflation, revive productivity, and restore incentives without making economic inequality worse among occupational groups and cities and villages.

Within the context of these enormous domestic difficulties, two developments must be clearly understood if the strategic value of China for America's Asian policy has any real importance. The first, as Chapter One by Ray S. Cline points out, is the strategy of relying upon China as a counterweight to offset the Soviet Union has backfired. Since Sino-American normalization, the Soviet Union has expanded its influence in Indochina and greatly strengthened its military forces in the Soviet Far East, not to mention the aggression in Afghanistan, to alter the current military balance of forces in Asia. When Soviet leaders expressed their distaste for the Washington-Beijing alliance, they promised to match it with appropriate means of their own. Consequently, they have initiated an escalation of military buildup and increased tensions in southwestern and northeastern Asia, as well as Southeast Asia.

The second development is the Washington-Beijing connection predicated on the American expectation that China will continue to remain an ally of the United States. There is little evidence to support this presumption. China's Marxist-Leninist party merely perceives the Soviet Union as more dangerous than the United States to its national security. This perception could change at any time. Moreover, if Beijing and Moscow agree to settle their border difficulties and expand trade and peoples' exchange, what will Washington do?

China also has interests in Asia that clash with our own, making the current alliance far from credible. On more than one occasion Beijing has reminded the world that it intends to resolve the Taiwan question on its own terms, even if that requires force. Although China has reduced its assistance to friendly groups in Southeast Asia, it still intends to expand its influence in the region and still takes every opportunity to use its friends—communist guerrillas in Burma, Thailand, or Malaysia, and its overseas Chinese networks—to advance its interests. Also, China has tried to drive a wedge between Japan and the Soviet Union by such diplomatic maneuvers as insisting that the 1978 Sino-Japanese Peace Treaty make reference to outsiders seeking "hegemony in the Asian-Pacific region."

Sino-American friendship must be built step by step by proven trust and confidence that will take many years to achieve. Meanwhile, until there is more proof of such trust, the United States would best be advised to be cautious in its relations with China.

A Summing Up

In either virulent, muted, or latent form, four kinds of conflict exist in Asia that could tip the balance of power and endanger peace and security. First, violent military-political struggle, within a state or between states, is now taking place in Afghanistan between Muslim rebels and the Soviet-backed regime of Babrak Karmal. Fighting continues in Kampuchea between the forces of Heng Samrin, aided by Vietnam and the Soviet Union, and the Khmer Rouge and its supporter, China; such violence can undermine regional balances of power. If the forces of Babrak Karmal routed the Muslim rebels and consolidated their power, Pakistan and other states would perceive an unfavorable balance of power. If the Khmer Rouge insurgents forced Heng Samrin's withdrawal from parts of Kampuchea, Vietnam would seek further Soviet assistance and possibly extend the war into Thailand to cut off supplies for the Khmer Rouge. Reacting to this power imbalance, one or more of the ASEAN states might join the war.

Second, acute tension exists along the borders of a number of Asian nations. Any action taken by these states to strengthen their borders, acquire advanced technology from either of the superpowers, or claim resources contested by another state would be perceived by the other as upsetting the political equilibrium. Historical precedents are the pre-emptive attack of the north against the south on the Korean peninsula in June 1950 and China's attack on Vietnam in February 1979.

Third, a state of internal war exists in the Philippines, Indonesia, Burma, Thailand, and Malaysia—nations in the process of modernization. Although such conflicts are limited to communist guerrillas, Muslim fundamentalist activists, or ethnic separatists demanding political independence, they threaten the political stability of the states. Created by rapid modernization, a variety of other strains and tensions also exist. If these governments fall, the succeeding powers might choose a different relationship with Moscow, Beijing, or Washington, thus altering the status quo.

Finally, conflict might originate at any time between states in their search for oil under the sea, from trade dumping that threatens domestic industries, or the disclosure that a neighbor has developed an atomic bomb. Such potential conflicts could strain international relations and force some states to seek new alliances, thus upsetting the regional power balance.

During the past three years, U.S. policies of giving top priority to Western Europe, relying upon China to counterbalance the Soviet Union in Asia, rearming Japan, and transferring modern weapons and economic aid to such states as Pakistan have not effectively dealt with these threats of conflict. But these conflicts persist and threaten to engulf neighboring states; tensions have worsened rather than improved. The Soviet presence in Asia is now greater than it was three years ago. Since U.S. foreign policy in Asia took shape under the Carter administration and received impetus during the first year of President Reagan's administration, the situation in Asia has deteriorated.

A number of countries must make difficult choices between allocating more scarce resources for defense or for social and economic development. Either choice might produce domestic instability, increased tensions or war with another state. America's current Asian policy unnecessarily pressures Asian leaders to make risky choices that might produce unintended consequences. Furthermore, this same policy leads to excessive dependency upon China, which is a most uncertain and as yet unproven ally. For these reasons, this volume of essays offers an alternative policy for the United States to pursue in Asia.

Elements of a New American Policy in Asia

Four key principles underscore this new policy:

— Recognize that Asia's strategic importance is as great as Western Europe's;

— Develop multiple country-by-country linkages with the Asian Pacific-basin countries;

— Elevate India's importance to a level equivalent to China's in America's Asian policy; and

— Maintain a strong American naval and air force presence in the Indian and Pacific oceans and enlist our Asian allies to cooperate and support efforts to deploy and effectively use that military power to guarantee freedom of the seas.

Let us examine each of these principles and then take all four together as components of a policy to deal with the critical conflicts and problem areas already described.

Long familiar with viewing the world solely from a European perspective, America's leaders still underrate the importance of Asia for influencing world affairs. This attitude is curious given U.S. involvement in three Asian wars since 1940. As Donald C. Hellmann shows in Chapter Five, those wars produced a profound sense of frustration and failure in America, which is perhaps responsible for the continuation of our fixation upon the West. Our so-called policing actions in Korea and Vietnam were never resolved to dramatize any victory. The emotional fallout from those conflicts weakened America's will and accelerated a move toward a policy of improving relations with China. Asia's diverse cultures and different values and behavior have never been viewed with empathy by U.S. leaders. By attributing qualities to Asians that Asians only partially share, Americans have continually misjudged Asian conduct and ideas.

Although there is no easy way to correct these perceptions, a step in the right direction would be to recognize that events in Asia are going to affect America's national security and fortunes as much as events in Bonn, Paris, or Rome. Hellmann iterates a theme echoed in all the chapters of this volume: America must become as sensitive to Asia's strategic importance as it is to Europe's strategic importance.

The Asian Pacific-basin states include Japan, South Korea, Taiwan, the ASEAN countries of Singapore, Malaysia, Thailand, Indonesia, and the Philippines, Australia, and New Zealand. During the 1970s these Asian Pacific-basin countries were the most rapidly growing economies in the world, and in 1979 American imports from that bloc exceeded imports from Western Europe. American exports to the Asian Pacific basin were nearly $40 billion in U.S. dollars compared to almost $54 billion to Western Europe; the region has nearly achieved economic equivalence with Western Europe for the United States.

There is every reason to expect that per capita income for this region will surge upward in the 1980s. Some countries such as Japan and possibly South Korea and Taiwan might even leap beyond their current stage into the postindustrial society by the end of this century. Such a leap would be signified by the employment of instantaneous information systems in both the public and private sectors and the increased productivity of the service sector of the economy.

In spite of their different cultures, the countries of this region share some important attributes with the West. They respect private property and encourage the freedom of the marketplace. These states also tolerate diverse associations at the grass roots so long as they do not act to subvert the political system. Finally, these countries permit and tolerate a wide range of diverse intellectual and cultural activities.

By suggesting that the United States forge closer ties with these countries, we are arguing that America should build from the present great strengths of those states that share similar interests with America. Improving bilateral and multilateral ties with these states will enable the United States to encourage greater foreign trade and increase the flow of American capital into the region. The Soviet Union should perceive that such a development poses no threat to its Asian frontiers and even offers that country expanded opportunities for trade and investment, which might help defuse regional tensions.

The third element, upgrading India's strategic importance for the United States, deserves serious consideration, as the chapters by Walter K. Andersen and Leo E. Rose cogently argue. Simply stated, American policymakers have refused to take seriously India's unique geographic location and the Indian Ocean's strategic importance for the United States. More serious is the legacy of misunderstanding and confused perceptions shared by India and the United States since the early 1950s. Rather than consulting to find ways to cooperate, each has castigated or ignored the other while improving relations with third parties regarded as dangerous to the security of India or the United States.

India is the major economic and military power in south Asia. Further, it has considerable influence with Third World countries through its leadership role in the Nonalignment Movement, which met at Havana in 1979 and in New Delhi in 1981. With its border on the Indian Ocean, India's support is vital for any nation interested in maintaining a naval presence there. Finally, India has lately created strong domestic foundations to become a formidable economic and military power by the end of this century.

For these reasons, the United States should strive to cultivate good relations with this growing giant. Although some in Washington might hesitate because of Soviet-Indian friendship ties, as Leo Rose points out, strains already have developed between New Delhi and Moscow, and those friendly ties are much exaggerated. What Washington must strive to accomplish is an improvement in Indian-Pakistani relations, certainly no easy task, but this tactic could gradually diminish Soviet influence in both countries. In other words, Washington policymakers should reassess the strategic importance of India by improving ties with that country and trying to strengthen the south Asian security system in order to counter Soviet influence in that region.

Such a security system, however, will depend upon American naval strength, and American naval power is now stretched to the limit, operating in the Pacific, Indian, and Atlantic oceans and the Mediterranean Sea. The U.S. Navy is in desperate need of being increased and outfitted with a variety of surface ships for both attack and self-support to ensure the freedom of maritime commerce. Access to the Persian Gulf for oil is essential for all industrial countries, and the Asian Pacific-basin countries are particularly vulnerable if the vital choke points in Southeast Asian waters are not protected. These countries depend upon freedom of the seas for their trade, and their assistance is vital for helping the U.S. Navy and Air Force to monitor shipping lines and maintain the flow of Middle East oil.

The exemplary bilateral relations of ANZUS—Australia, New Zealand, and the United States—ought to serve as a model for how such cooperation could be established between the United States and the Asian Pacific-basin countries. As Chapter Six by Henry S. Albinski shows, Australia and New Zealand have not antagonized their Asian neighbors; their leaders still recognize the strategic importance of their countries for the United States and have cautiously acted in their mutual interests. Through mutual consultation, the three countries have developed reciprocal means for protecting the national security of each.

Australia has supplied the Untied States with navigational and space-tracking facilities, and U.S. B-52s based in Guam are permitted to transit occasionally in Australia by way of Darwin. Besides providing the United States with access to the region, Australia and New Zealand have a small, high-quality military capability, which can be deployed to supplement American fighting forces at an appropriate time. Both countries have also cooperated with ASEAN and have good relations with China and India; thus, they have supported the United States in various ways through their bilateral ties with those Asian states. For example, they discouraged Tonga, Western Samoa, and the Cook Islands from granting the Soviets fishing access in exchange for Soviet assistance to develop their docks and airports. Finally, both countries have augmented American naval and air capabilities by providing critical information about sea traffic between the Pacific and Indian oceans and by persuading Singapore to serve as a new basing site for the United States.

The chapters in this volume will illustrate the components of an effective U.S. foreign policy for the 1980s and beyond in answer to this central question: Can taking Asia more seriously, developing closer ties with the Asian Pacific-basin states, improving ties with India, and maintaining a strong naval and air force presence in the Indian and Pacific oceans constitute a new Asian policy for America?

A U.S. Foreign Policy for Asia in the 1980s and Beyond

The agenda of security concerns for the United States in Asia in this decade and the next is to contain Soviet military expansion and influence, resolve the conflicts in Afghanistan and Kampuchea, and ease tensions between those states with long-standing border problems. Finding solutions for these problems may well restore and maintain the balance of power in Asia's geopolitical regions.

If the United States persists in its present course of allying with China and rearming Japan, future developments will be like those of the past three years, or possibly worse. The transfer of military-related technology and weaponry to China will not impress the Soviet Union and will only be countered by increased Soviet military buildup in the Far East. Rapid Japanese rearmament would similarly trigger a Soviet buildup and worry South

Korea, the ASEAN states, and Australia and New Zealand. Following the Chinese foreign policy line in Indochina is a guarantee of perpetuating that regional conflict with the strong likelihood of involving Thailand as well. Transferring huge amounts of military and economic aid to Pakistan runs the grave risk of embroiling that country in the Afghan conflict and producing chaotic conditions on India's northwest border. The United States' current Asian policy, in other words, has an excellent chance of making conditions in Asia worse than they presently are.

A new policy is advocated in Chapter One by Ray Cline, who argues that the United States should adopt a far more cautious approach toward Beijing and, instead, more actively encourage trade, foreign investment, and technological exchange between the countries of the Asian Pacific basin. While promoting these same developments, the United States should also widely consult with friendly states in this region to map out a clear consensus of security concerns. The United States could assist its allies, and they in turn could provide some modest support for strengthening America's naval and air force capabilities in the Indian and Pacific oceans.

As the United States' ties with the Asian Pacific-basin countries become stronger, Sino-American relations will gradually develop by their own momentum and mutual confidence will grow. These actions should not be perceived by the Soviet Union as threatening its security, and the current military balance in northeast Asia might then be stabilized and maintained.

The policy of multiple linkages between Asian Pacific-basin countries and the United States takes another form in Chapter Seven by Franklin B. Weinstein. By assisting the Republic of Korea to develop a military independence from the United States by the end of the 1980s, Washington might also cooperate with Tokyo to widen channels of contact with North Korea while making absolutely certain that Seoul is consulted and approves of such moves. If both policies could be balanced with all states in agreement, America might gradually disengage militarily from South Korea and begin normalization with Pyongyang; at the same time, China and the Soviet Union might then be encouraged to normalize relations with Seoul. These developments would go far to reduce tensions on the Korean peninsula.

The continued prosperity and security of Taiwan is also critical for the peace and security of the Asian Pacific-basin states. The United States-Taiwan Relations Act presently allows the United States and Taiwan to conduct normal commercial treaties and engage in trade. This act permits America to sell military weapons to Taiwan to ensure that its sovereignty is upheld. This legislation also enables the United States to develop good relations with China and not become involved in any future negotiations or ties that Taiwan and China might initiate between each other.

xxiv | *Introduction*

This new policy of building upon the great strengths of the Asian Pacific-basin countries could then be extended toward improving relations with India, so that Washington could then initiate a series of diplomatic moves to calm the troubled waters in southern Asia. While negotiating with Pakistan on the aid it intends to supply over the next five years, Washington should consult with India and give it strong assurances that such aid will not be used to tip the balance of power between those two countries. At the same time, Washington could support its allies' desire to bring the Soviet Union to the bargaining table by pressing for a regional conference of India, China, Pakistan, and the USSR and by trying to break the deadlock over the participation of the Babrak Karmal regime as a condition for meeting. While improving its relations with New Delhi, Washington might be able to receive Indian support for establishing a powerful naval presence in the northwest Indian Ocean. To prevent the Soviet Union and Vietnam from enlarging their spheres of influence beyond the Indochina peninsula, the United States ought to elicit India's assistance to work with ASEAN to achieve a political settlement for resolving the present conflict in Kampuchea.

As those parties collaborate to find a settlement, the United States might try to persuade China to accept the current Indochinese status quo as an alternate way of weakening the Soviet strategic presence in Southeast Asia. Similarly, Washington could give assurances to Thai leaders of aid and military support in exchange for Bangkok's agreement to a Vietnamese-sponsored Kampuchean regime. These developments would be premised on an understanding with Hanoi that regional acceptance of its hegemonic position in Indochina must be accompanied by reduced Soviet military access to Vietnam's naval and air bases. Even if China failed to agree, Washington could still gradually disassociate from China's Indochina policy, as Sheldon W. Simon suggests in Chapter Four, and present an alternative to the ASEAN states.

This alternative would involve U.S. diplomatic maneuvers to line up all ASEAN states behind an acceptance of Vietnam's hegemony in Indochina, while encouraging ASEAN to take the lead in negotiating conditions for recognition with Hanoi. ASEAN would seek Hanoi's agreement to limit the total number of its military forces in Indochina and to withdraw them entirely from western Kampuchea. Hanoi would be asked to reduce its dependency upon Moscow and seek to build relations with neighboring and industrial countries. Here again, the good offices of India could be employed to persuade Hanoi to negotiate. Finally, diplomatic efforts should be made to limit Soviet use of Vietnamese bases as a part of the total package in exchange for which Japanese and Western European coffers would be opened for Indochina's reconstruction.

This new American policy toward Asia is, of course, predicated upon improved relations between the United States and Japan. The Reagan administration must resist any domestic pressures for greater tariff protection while encouraging the Japanese to open their doors for more American goods. More importantly, this new policy requires not stampeding the Japanese into rearmament. A great deal more consultation should take place between Tokyo and Washington to reach an agreement for a modest Japanese military supplement to assist the United States in the Pacific as well as to assume a greater burden of the costs for America's military forces in Japan. Such an agreement, moreover, must be based on similar perceptions of northeast Asia's security needs and how these relate to those of the United States and to other nations of the Pacific. Finally, this agreement ought to be tailored to meet Japan's domestic fiscal needs and its security concerns.

The United States should be able to initiate and carry out this new foreign policy toward Asia in the 1980s and beyond. This new policy should minimize conflict and tension in Asia and restore the balance of power there as well as improve relations between the two superpowers, the United States and the Soviet Union. The recommendations presented in this study are well within U.S. capabilities.

1 | U.S. FOREIGN POLICY FOR ASIA

Ray S. Cline

The whole world faces the 1980s in an anxious and uncertain mood. Multiple sources of economic dissatisfaction, political upheaval, and military insecurity confront nearly every nation, either within its own borders or in nearby states. As the Chinese Communists used to say only a few years ago, "there is a great disorder under heaven," a condition hailed by the late Chinese Premier Zhou Enlai because it ripened revolutionary situations for exploitation. Now Beijing's leaders are more sober and intent on maintaining stability as they seek financial and technological help from capitalist industrial countries to try to modernize their impoverished economy. They also look eagerly to the United States and its NATO allies to counter Soviet strategic pressures being felt everywhere, including eastern Asia and the western Pacific, the Asian Pacific basin.

During Ronald Reagan's first months in office, voices in nearly every foreign capital asked whether U.S. national power, particularly U.S. political will and coherence of strategic purpose, would be restored from the depths reached in the Carter administration. It is a challenging task because President Reagan must rebuild stability and confidence to levels adequate to restabilize international relations while avoiding either war or surrender in the United States' conflict with the Soviet Union.

The broad outlines of American foreign policy are beginning to take shape based on firm resistance to Soviet expansion of its sphere of domination. This resistance can be successful only if it is accompanied by U.S. economic revitalization and an alliance-oriented military buildup sufficient to deter the USSR's regional aggression. As usual, America's role in Asia is the vaguest and least predictable part of U.S. strategic thinking.

The Reagan administration has declared that Japan is a "pillar of American policy" in the Asian Pacific region. Today, the importance of closely coordinated Japanese-American relations is becoming clear to leaders of government not only in the White House but also on Capitol Hill. The United States is determined to remain a Pacific power, politically, economically, and strategically. The success of U.S. policy in Asia, indeed in the whole world, depends upon the continuance of strong ties with Japan, a nation towering over all others in the Asian Pacific community.

The United States and Japan formally linked their strategic fortunes in an interdependent security association in 1952, during the period of the Korean War. The current Treaty of Mutual Cooperation and Security between the two nations, ratified on June 23, 1960, specified reciprocal obligations on the part of the military forces of Japan and the United States "to resist attack" and work together for the "maintenance of international peace and security." Bound by a common concern for the safety and welfare of the Japanese and American people, the partnership has grown ever deeper, more productive in cultural and technological contacts, and more steadfast in facing security dangers as they have mounted in the Pacific and elsewhere.

The primary threat to the noncommunist states of the western Pacific and to the United States is the persistent strengthening of Soviet military forces in Asia. In addition to stationing 45 ground divisions on the Sino-Soviet border, the USSR has recently deployed surface combatants as well as ballistic-missile submarines to its already large Pacific fleet, occupied former American air bases at Da Nang and former naval facilities at Cam Ranh Bay in Vietnam, garrisoned division-size ground forces on the islands of Japan's Northern Territories, and introduced SS-20 intermediate-range missiles and long-range bombers to the Asian Pacific basin. This regional buildup of Soviet military might marks the beginning of a new strategic era. Soviet activities and maneuvers with increasing numbers of modern ships and aircraft have a direct effect on the U.S.-USSR military balance of power in the western Pacific and worldwide, particularly in view of the reduction of U.S. naval and air units for operations in the Indian Ocean.

It is striking that war and the threat of war disrupt the communist world even more than they disrupt the free world. In the Asian Pacific basin, rivalry between the two communist giants—the Soviet Union and the People's Republic of China (PRC)—makes the area potentially disruptive and explosive. The leaders of the communist bloc are determined to advance communist power to new heights domestically and into new territories externally, never doubting—at least not publicly—that their aim is to establish either a Marxist-Leninist or a Marxist-Leninist-Maoist system of government that eventually would spread across the whole globe.

Communist China considers itself the ultimate central kingdom of world communist states and, as such, the greatest power on earth. The Oriental time frame is long and Chinese patience and endurance are great. Still, within its limited capacities, Beijing acts now as the main Asian strategic antagonist of the USSR. The very existence of China complicates every calculation in Moscow and Washington, although there are serious doubts in both capitals as to how and when China will be able to reach the ambitious goals it has set for itself. In pursuit of security in Asia, Beijing has turned with increasing importunity to support from the United States.

When President Jimmy Carter and Vice-Premier Deng Xiaoping met in Washington during the first weeks of 1979, the two leaders celebrated the opening of full diplomatic relations between China and the United States. Each leader was thinking of his own private dream about the personal political prestige and the national strategic benefits of the new relationship between the two countries. The rhetoric was the same, the strategic goals were quite dissimilar. As the Chinese say of any kind of ill-conceived match or alliance, "same beds, different dreams."

Carter was elated over the psychological pressure he believed his playing the "China card" would put on Moscow to restrain its increasingly active expansion in Southeast Asia, the Middle East, and Africa. He thought normalization of diplomatic relations with China would be popular not only with critics urging a firmer foreign policy but also with American business leaders hoping for a bonanza in trade with China.

Deng was elated because he now could "teach Vietnam a lesson" by a military attack without risking direct Soviet retaliation. He also thought his playing the "American card" would bring vast dollar investment and modern technology to China's primitive and faltering economy. In this way he could confound his domestic enemies by getting the capitalists to subsidize his program of the "four modernizations"—agriculture, industry, science and technology, and military forces.

In television spectaculars and other diplomatic ritual performances in Washington, Deng and Carter repeated that normalization would advance world peace and enhance stability in east Asia. President Carter solemnly declared, "We've charted a new and irreversible course toward a firmer, more constructive, and a more hopeful relationship." Vice-Premier Deng expressed thanks "for the many friendly words" from Americans initiating an era of close cooperation "between our two countries and our two peoples."[1]

There was no mention anywhere at the time that China is a politically oppressive one-party dictatorship governing one billion desperately poor

Asian people with too few resources to raise standards of living much or easily in the next few decades. No one commented that the United States, in contrast to China, is the richest pluralist society in the world, leading a voluntary alliance of states determined to keep their political liberties and independence in the face of military and political pressures from the Soviet Union, a nation whose political system and ideology are almost identical with those of mainland China.

The foreign policy of quasi-alliance thus hinted at between the United States and China was well calculated to irritate Soviet geopoliticians. At present the USSR is not afraid of Chinese military forces, which are extremely large but technologically primitive and many years away from any real modernization at the American or Soviet level of combat capability. Looking at the future in the longer run, the Soviets have a paranoid fear of the enormous Chinese population on the 4,500-mile border of their comparatively empty Siberian and Far East hinterland, on whose raw material resources they are counting in the years to come. The fact that many of the people on the Soviet side of the border do not share the ethnic and cultural background of Slavic Russians exacerbates Soviet fears.

The principal and compelling aim of U.S. foreign policy in the Asian Pacific basin for the 1980s, therefore, ought to be to move definitively away from the tinsel dream of blocking the aggressive policies of the USSR by linking American strategy to the dreams of Deng Xiaoping. His unrealistic dreams are already coming dangerously close to collapsing. China is in no sense a superpower nor is it a reliable long-term ally of the United States. Puncturing the myths of commonality of interest between Beijing and Washington created by the pro-Beijing lobby and President Carter is the first task of the foreign policymakers of the Reagan administration. Since many officials sympathetic to closer ties with China are still in place in the foreign affairs bureaucracy and the public orchestration of opinion by the Chinese embassy is extremely effective with intellectuals and writers, the task will not be easy.

There are joint interests and advantages to be pursued with China on a quid pro quo basis insofar as practicable, and the United States should consult cooperatively and prudently to do so. As President Reagan said during the 1980 campaign, he wants to extend the hand of friendship to Chinese everywhere. On the other hand, Washington cannot become a captive of Beijing's strategic planners. The United States must base its main policy thrust in east and Southeast Asia on strengthening the remarkably promising ties that have grown up bilaterally, and in some ways multilaterally, among the United States and the ten noncommunist states in the western Pacific.

After many years of diplomatic separation, the reuniting of the United States and the People's Republic of China at the ambassadorial level stimulated an abundance of fanciful theories of political and strategic advantages stemming from normalization. Some flourished in China, others in the United States. Most are ill-founded myths that never had a chance of success. The most significant ones are based on belief that China would quickly overcome its difficulties at home and abroad and assume a prominent role as a stabilizing political and economic force in Asia. One might hope that this prospect could materialize. To rely on this hope for the 1980s, however, is folly for American policymakers, as events so far have indicated. The first item on the Reagan foreign policy agenda for Asia ought to be to puncture three debilitating myths now widely accepted.

Myth One

The first myth, voiced in official circles in America during the Carter administration and still persisting, is that the 1979 U.S. tilt toward China would strengthen the U.S. strategic posture and inhibit Soviet advances in eastern Asia. Zbigniew Brzezinski, assistant to the president for national security affairs, said, "Few actions will contribute more to the security and stability of our important positions around the rim of Asia...than a constructive involvement with China."[2]

In fact, for the short term at least, U.S. positions on the periphery of Asia have deteriorated in the past two years. This is because the language used by many U.S. officials gave Moscow reason to fear that the United States had finally and formally combined forces with the Soviet Union's bitterest antagonist, China, in a united front with a long-term military thrust against the USSR. Soviet President Leonid Brezhnev reacted with strong reservations about U.S. intentions when Carter moved abruptly to end the 30-year policy of opposition or cautious distance in dealing with the mainland regime.

Soviet leaders immediately charged, with some justice, that "the Americans doubtless are viewing normalization of their relations with the PRC as a lever for pressure on the Soviet Union."[3] They lost no time in staging countermoves worldwide, including critical steps in Southeast Asia, designed to continue advancement toward what they call an "irreversible gain in the correlation of forces"—a decisive shift of world power away from China and the United States and its allies.

In the Pacific area within a few weeks, Soviet naval and air forces began using the elaborate former U.S. base facilities at Cam Ranh Bay and Da Nang in Vietnam, and they provided extensive logistical support for the

Vietnamese armies in the defensive battles against the Chinese attack across the border, as well as for the 200 thousand men of the Vietnamese invasion and military occupation of Democratic Kampuchea (Cambodia).[4]

During 1980 the USSR also turned its attention to increasing its air and ground defense on the Kurile Islands north of Japan[5] (occupied by the USSR at the end of World War II), and to improving Soviet ties with North Korea.[6] To the south it began patrolling the South China Sea and the Strait of Malacca with attack submarines.[7] The Soviets encircled China while threatening the sea-lanes throughout the western Pacific.

At the Kremlin's Palace of Congresses in Moscow, Brezhnev boasted before the Central Committee of the Communist Party in February 1981 of "further growth in the might, activity, and prestige of the Soviet Union" and cooperation with "other countries of the socialist community" in "building a new socialist world." He went on to say that "the sphere of imperialist domination of the world has narrowed" and warned against American "aggressiveness" in countering this trend. He especially viewed with alarm the U.S.-China connection: "There is a simple calculation behind the readiness of the United States, Japan, and a number of NATO countries to expand military-political ties with China, that of exploiting its hostility to the Soviet Union and to the socialist community in their own imperialist interests."[8]

The Chinese Communists, for their part, never lose an opportunity to accuse Brezhnev of steadily pursuing his strategic target of world hegemony. Never do they moderate their views on the likelihood that "the polar bear to the north" will initiate World War III. After the Soviet invasion of Afghanistan at the end of 1979, China announced that Beijing was breaking off discussions with the USSR since it was inappropriate given the circumstances to hold Sino-Soviet negotiations for improvement in relations between the two nations.[9]

These regional moves to incorporate large slices of the Asian Pacific basin into the Soviet political, economic, and strategic sphere have been supplemented by a substantial buildup of the USSR's Pacific naval and air forces in the Vladivostok and Petropavlovsk-Kamchatskiy regions of the Soviet maritime provinces.

Asian concern about the USSR and its ally, Vietnam, runs from Japan and South Korea through the Strait of Malacca, to Indonesia, Malaysia, Singapore, across to Thailand, and down to Australia and New Zealand. On January 15, 1979, when Brzezinski proposed that normalization of relations with China would, in part, consolidate the balance of power in east Asia, he could not have anticipated the succession of Soviet aggressive moves that have taken place. Instead of intimidating or deterring the Soviet Union, the

U.S. policy of normalizing relations with China has resulted in a shift in the east Asian balance of power adverse to U.S. interests. This is the reality that has emerged, a reality that now must be met with effective measures to deter its continuation on present lines of development.

Myth Two

The second myth, also still widely held in official Washington circles, is that China is a loyal friend, virtually an ally, of the United States. This has never been true, not even at the time of Carter's joyful greeting to Deng at the end of January 1979. The friendliness of China consisted mainly of deemphasizing standard Maoist hostile propaganda attacks against the "American imperialists." The basic values and goals of the Chinese communist society remain fundamentally incompatible with the aims and interests of the United States.

The constitution of the Chinese Communist Party, approved unanimously by the Eleventh National Congress on August 18, 1977, is still in force. Deng Xiaoping had already returned to a position of power at the time the constitution was adopted. It proclaims that the party "unites with the proletariat, the oppressed people and nations of the world and fights shoulder to shoulder with them to oppose the hegemonism of the two superpowers, the Soviet Union and the United States, to overthrow imperialism, modern revisionism, and all reaction."[10]

Prior to the adoption of the constitution, Premier Hua Guofeng candidly explained that the United States is the less dangerous of China's two main enemies. "The Soviet Union and the United States are the source of a new world war, and Soviet social imperialism, in particular, presents the greater danger." Quoting Lenin admiringly, he continued, "The more powerful enemy can be vanquished . . . by taking advantage of every, even the smallest, opportunity of gaining a mass ally, even though this ally is temporary, vacillating, unstable, unreliable, and conditional."[11] Here, plainly, is the role in which Beijing sees the United States—temporarily. This is the friendship that Carter was so proud to have won.

These sentiments—spelled out so meticulously in the Communist Party's constitution—remain in the minds of the Chinese leaders today. Vice-Premier Deng embroidered them in explaining his willingness to join ranks with the United States, the weaker of the two enemies, to bring down the USSR. The Chinese have never claimed common interests with Americans, merely the possibility of parallel courses of action. Furthermore, in the face of U.S. insistence on no use of military force against Taiwan, Beijing's firm position is, as Deng said, that "Taiwan must be liberated, it being only a question of time ... Eventually it will have to be done through military action."[12]

To make certain that the USSR completely understood the shift in strategic emphasis to an anti-Soviet front with the United States, the Chinese Communists insisted that the joint communiqué establishing diplomatic relations with the United States make clear that "each is opposed to efforts by any other country or group of countries to establish ... hegemony in the Asia Pacific region or in any other region of the world."[13] Beijing could not have been disappointed by Moscow's fiery response that the hegemony concept was an excuse for creating an anti-Soviet alliance. Whether or not Washington officials understood what was happening, giving the impression that such an alliance was being formed was exactly what Vice-Premier Deng had in mind.

What Deng had promised his people at home was "mainly know-how and equipment in the scientific and technological fields which would be most beneficial to our realization of the four modernizations."[14] In justifying his own switch to cooperate with Washington he said, "At present, they have something to ask from us, and we hold the complete initiative in dealing with them."[15] A full eighteen months after concluding normalization procedures with the United States, Deng still thought it important to find an occasion to say that "it is not quite appropriate" to call the United States an ally.[16]

Myth Three

The third myth that must be punctured is that Vice-Premier Deng has firm control of a stable regime in Beijing—one that is able to work with a unity of purpose in a comparatively democratic style to lift China promptly out of poverty and backwardness. It was claimed that diplomatic recognition of China would usher in a new era of constructive political and economic relations with the United States.

Then, inevitably, some skepticism began to creep into comments in both capitals, Beijing and Washington. In 1980 Deng began reshuffling China's leadership in internal political purges designed to secure sufficient backing for his lagging program of the four modernizations.[17]

In addition, he demanded that Democracy Wall, which for a few months so impressed foreign journalists as a harbinger of democratic freedom, be closed by law, removing it from the constitutional list of rights. Most important, Deng decided that the Gang of Four, led by Jiang Qing (Mao Zedong's widow), be brought to trial for treason, thus tending to discredit not only Mao but Deng's nominal superior, Hua Guofeng, and the millions of his supporters who came into office between 1966 and 1976, when Deng was in disgrace. Jiang Qing's defiance of Deng and the purge trial court, plus her reprieve from execution, suggested that Deng was not totally on firm political ground.

Finally, and most notably from the United States' point of view, Deng began warning Washington against continuing U.S. economic and security commitments to Taiwan as a political entity separate from the mainland, as required by the Taiwan Relations Act passed by the U.S. Congress and signed into law in 1979. Three days before President Ronald Reagan's inauguration, the Beijing newspaper *Zhongguo Qingnian Bao* voiced China's official warning: "If the United States should develop once again the 'two China' or 'one China and one Taiwan' policy today, it will definitely lead to a retrogression in Sino-American relations."[18] Yet the actual situation confronting foreign nations is the de facto existence, side by side, of two antagonistic social and political systems, one ruled from Beijing and the other from Taipei. There is only one Chinese civilization, one Chinese culture, and one Chinese ethnic identity, but there are in reality two separate Chinese political bodies claiming sovereignty. Only by brutally forcing 18 million Chinese people on Taiwan to submit unwillingly to communist domination could the United States comply with Beijing's wishes. Deng cannot win on this issue. His need to inflate the issue of Taiwan suggests weakness and a lack of confidence in China's ability to manipulate American leaders in support of Chinese aims in Asia.

The greatest threat to political stability in China, however, is that since normalization of diplomatic relations with the United States, Deng's program of the four modernizations has made little or no progress. His regime has now been forced to admit to what it calls "leftist" errors in the management of the economy. As a result, Beijing acknowledges, inflation is high and the budget is unbalanced, something Mao never would have openly confessed. In addition, the regime recently has been pointing directly at the United States and Western Europe for a large part of the failure. "At present, those without strong willpower within the ranks of our party have already been corrupted by the bad influence from outside," was the opinion of a party secretary published in *Renmin Ribao* in February 1981. "The bad influence of bourgeois ideas and a decadent way of life is sweeping like a wind everywhere," the official party paper revealed. "We must work in concert with relevant departments to resist this bad influence from outside."[19]

To make matters worse, a United Nations' fact-finding mission reported in early March of 1981 that a combination of flooding in the south and drought in the north has caused millions of peasants to suffer from hunger, severe malnutrition, and infectious diseases. In good years, when there are increases in grain production per unit area, China has admitted that per capita grain output is only approximately equivalent to that of 1957. According to figures released in Beijing, the average per capita gross national product (GNP) in 1979 was only $253, resulting in a standard of living that has not risen much, if any, above levels of 25 years ago.[20] Even if earnings are somewhat larger, perhaps $400 or $500 in U.S. dollars, as American sinologists think, the economic record is very poor. Visitors to the countryside see little change in the remoter villages from the subsistence conditions they knew in the 1930s.[21]

Vice-Premier Yao Yilin now speaks of 800 million peasants making no real contribution to the economy and has confirmed that China is obliged to delay by two or three more years much progress on Deng's program of the four modernizations, which was launched with fanfare of being within easy reach when diplomatic relations with the United States were normalized. Retrenchment has caused the cancellation of billions of dollars of contracts with foreign firms, especially Japanese and American, due to euphoric miscalculations by Chinese economic planners in 1979 and 1980.

Disappointment runs deep not only with foreign investors but also with the Chinese themselves. In comparing how economic affairs were handled on the mainland with how they were handled by the leaders on Taiwan, Vice-Premier Yu Qiuli moaned, "While we were rapidly regressing, they suddenly forged rapidly, even miraculously, ahead. With the one in high gear and the other moving backward, the gap continued widening until we were forced to pull our heads out of the sand and admit that we had lost in this bloodless war of peaceful economic competition."[22] China does not exhibit much confidence in the method of retrieving itself by "criticism and self-criticism," as Deng proposed at the central party work conference at the end of 1980.[23] The other way out is to seize control of the dynamic Taiwan economy by political skill or military force, hence the movement of the Taiwan issue off the back burner it usually occupies in stabler political times.

Furthermore, it is not clear that China has the administrative skills and political motivation under any program to create a unity of purpose and to hoist its subsistence-level economy out of poverty within the next twenty years. The present political and economic situation on the mainland vividly exposes the painful gap between Deng's promises and his performance, leaving him increasingly vulnerable to his many domestic enemies. The post-Mao succession struggle is not yet finally settled. The relationship with the United States is subject to sudden derangement as a result of shifts in the power struggle going on in Beijing.

Asian Realities

The reality on the mainland, quite different from the myths so sedulously cultivated in recent years, is that the communist regime is experiencing difficulties so great in many fields that Vice-Premier Deng has been obliged to fall back on instituting a "spiritual campaign" to overcome them; this term evokes Mao. Despite the shortcomings evidenced during its more than 30 years in power, the party continues to claim that "history will prove that socialism is the only road for the social development of mankind."[24] The record of the past two decades in east and Southeast Asia simply makes nonsense of this statement. The slogan is more reminiscent of Mao than the pragmatic reform policies, which have made Deng famous and, for a time, popular. Yet there is no other way for China to move without totally destroying its legitimacy.

The other four Asian communist countries also present a depressing scene. The Democratic People's Republic of Korea is frozen in mobilized military antagonism against the Republic of Korea to the south. The strategic dominoes, so scornfully dismissed as nonexistent by liberal critics of U.S. involvement in the Vietnam War, did in fact tumble in Laos and Kampuchea. Both are now under Hanoi's heavy military thumb. Thailand and Malaysia are apprehensive lest the fallout extend to their countryside, where for decades communist guerrillas have been trying to overthrow the governments.

The North Vietnamese who occupied South Vietnam in 1975 brutalized the people, as their pitiful flight by boats amply demonstrated. They set up a puppet communist government in Laos and another in Kampuchea. About 35 million Vietnamese, Lao, and Khmer who wanted nothing to do with the austere communist military dictatorship in North Vietnam have been brought into a semicolonial status under Hanoi's occupation. Several million died in the process. The result is not good from anybody's viewpoint. All of the Indochina peninsula is impoverished, hungry, and politically oppressed. The struggle for control in Kampuchea is still unresolved, and Vietnamese troops will probably stay there in force as long as guerrilla resistance continues.

About 80 million people live in these four small communist states—North Korea, Vietnam, Laos, and Kampuchea—and half of the population is under 30 years of age. All of the regimes have turned in dismal performances in their efforts to improve standards of living. What was only a while ago heralded as the wave of the future is a sluggish backwater and swamp.

The Emerging Pacific Community

In contrast with the bleak outlook of the Asian communist countries, the ten noncommunist Asian nations in the western Pacific are entering the 1980s in a new spirit of confidence, greater political stability, and remarkably dynamic growth. These ten are sometimes described as "the emerging Pacific community," a useful term for Japan, South Korea, Taiwan, for the Philippines, Indonesia, Singapore, Malaysia, and Thailand—the Association of Southeast Asian Nations—and for Australia and New Zealand. Collectively these ten constitute a significant grouping of international power. The total territory they encompass is nearly 4.5 million square miles. Within their boundaries live 450 million people—twice the number in the United States.

The phenomenal industrial growth of Japan, South Korea, and Taiwan has been accompanied by rapid development of the abundant raw material resources—oil, uranium, iron ore, tin, rubber, and foodstuffs—of Southeast Asia, Australia, and New Zealand. The interconnections and long-range business commitments among these economies are beginning to be as complex and sophisticated as those of Europe. Multinational investments, bilateral trade and banking arrangements, and increasing contacts among regional institutions, enterprising business leaders, and government planners are creating growing regional interdependence, as well as multiple links with the United States.

The result is that in 1980, the last year for which reliable statistics for all the countries are available, the GNP of these ten Pacific nations was about $1.8 trillion (by American calculations in U.S. 1980 dollars). It has since, of course, become considerably higher. Total trade between this region and the United States is now in the neighborhood of $110 billion, more than U.S. trade with the European community and about one-fourth of U.S. world trade.[25]

The ten noncommunist Asian nations, in particular the ASEAN members, all consciously and firmly limit their avowed common purposes to regional economic goals. Nevertheless, the extent and frequency of consultation and informal cooperation among them is staggering in view of their divergent ethnic, religious, and political backgrounds. In the past few years they have substantially increased their sophistication about strategy toward those continental Asian states that seek greater influence over their neighbors.

This more acute realism derives in part from the fact that most of these ten countries have crucial bilateral security arrangements with the United States. Taiwan, South Korea, Japan, the Philippines, Australia, and New

Zealand all have formal American treaties or legally binding commitments. Thailand relies heavily on vague but long-standing and credible U.S. assurances of assistance in the event of attack from Vietnam. The other three ASEAN governments—Indonesia, Malaysia, and Singapore—are increasingly aware that it is American military power that guarantees the safety of the sea-lanes along which all Pacific trade passes, including the oil tankers plying to and from the Indian Ocean. Some of these nations are formally nonaligned, but they all know that their strategic interests lie within their own emerging community and with the United States.

If the era of guilt about Vietnam is ending in the United States, as it seems to be with the election of President Reagan, it is high time. Hostility toward Americans has dissipated long since in the region where the real damage occurred. After all, most of the destruction took place after U.S. withdrawal rather than because of U.S. intervention. Perhaps some day disenchantment with the doctrinaire Communists and a yearning for a better life evident in the capitalist trading nations of the Pacific will bring about a stabilizing political fix, even in such strife-torn nations as Kampuchea.

American Strategy and Foreign Policy

Whatever the United States does or refrains from doing in eastern and Southeast Asia materially affects the fate of nations and people whose welfare is tied to U.S. fortunes, economically, politically, or militarily through dependence on American military strength for security. By and large, if U.S. military power is adequate and can be deployed where it is needed on the shores of the western Pacific to deter aggression and guarantee security, this region's economic prosperity and growth will create an environment permitting political equilibrium, civil liberties, and cultural benefits.

The goal of U.S. foreign policy ought to be an energetic, reinvigorated cooperation among the Asian states whose political ideology, economic health, and strategic security are in accord with U.S. interests. This means access to bases, deployment of air power, and, above all, the mobility and superior strength of U.S. naval forces to ensure peaceful interaction in the western Pacific. The main strategic task of the United States must be to protect in peace or in war the sea-lanes linking the trading nations of east Asia to one another, not only the advanced industrial nations but also the indispensable suppliers of raw material resources. Essentially what is called for is guaranteed safe passage either by sea or air along all international routes, especially through the strategic choke points where straits or narrow sea passages might permit blockage or harassment of traffic.

With such cooperation with one another and with the United States, the

Asian Pacific-basin states could go on with their common business in the economic confidence engendered by security. If the favorable trends in the emerging Pacific community persist and grow, the balance of power will gradually shift in a direction advantageous to the United States. The People's Republic of China, the giant communist state in the region, may assume some special association with the community if the Beijing regime can patch together a peaceful and stable relationship with its neighbors and maintain a cooperative attitude toward the United States. This remains to be seen.

What is remarkable now is that extraordinarily efficient and far-sighted leaders in east Asia—men like Chiang Ching-kuo of Taiwan, Chun Doo Hwan of South Korea, and Lee Kuan-yew of Singapore—are quietly working together to build economic strength and deter military encroachment. If their luck holds and they continue to cooperate with one another, the Pacific ten can transform east Asia into a zone of stability and prosperity. They will then serve as a barrier to further communist expansion, and indeed, their success will beckon to the communist five—China, North Korea, Vietnam, Kampuchea, and Laos—to stop their costly rivalries and turn away from the Soviet model toward open societies. If this happens in the long run, it will be the magnetic pull of the successful Pacific states that changes the balance of power back toward the pluralist nations looking to the United States for leadership. Creating the circumstances in which such a magnetic force can operate ought to be the main thrust of U.S. foreign policy in Asia in the 1980s.

The time has come for President Reagan to enunciate and rouse the people of the nation in support of a broad strategic concept based on resisting communist expansion, supporting friends and allies, expanding economic technology and world trade, and maintaining military parity plus naval superiority. The horizons of such an America, with its spiritual frontiers at the most distant edges of the three great oceans, are ample enough to charge our people with the feeling of national purpose, which has been feeble and uncertain since the twin tragedies of the defeat in Vietnam and the political collapse in Washington.

Today, the United States is widely perceived as exerting a stabilizing and civilizing force, bringing trade and prosperity, and comporting itself in a comparatively benign way throughout east Asia. Certainly in Southeast Asia, the most troubled and diverse region, even former enemies are disposed to welcome U.S. strategic presence and woo American help. This is good news for President Reagan. His foreign policy needs only to recognize that in Asia, as elsewhere, security and prosperity go hand in hand, and nothing succeeds like success.

The U.S. foreign policy must be based on the explicit premise that the

Leninist-Maoist system of militarized, overcentralized bureaucratic government set up in North Korea, the People's Republic of China, and the Indochinese states is a failure. The main thrust of American policy in east and Southeast Asia ought to be to consult closely and cooperate enthusiastically with the east Asian model of political organization that works—the "capitalist-road" nations. The Pacific ten, fully supported but in no way dominated by the United States, can tip the worldwide balance of power toward the open societies through developing international trade and mutual diplomatic cooperation in support of common security interests. The dynamic growth of these friendly Asian states provides the United States with the opportunity to build a firm and successful foreign policy in this part of the world, contributing toward redressing the U.S.-Soviet strategic balance in the crucial years of global tension in the 1980s and beyond.

Notes

1. "Transcript of Remarks Made by President Carter and Deputy Prime Minister Teng Hsiao-ping [Deng Xiaoping] in Washington," on January 31, 1979, *New York Times,* February 1, 1979.

2. "Remarks of Dr. Zbigniew Brzezinski, Assistant to the President for National Security Affairs, to Members of the National Council for U.S./China Trade and the USA/ROC Economic Council," *Release,* Office of the White House Press Secretary, January 15, 1979.

3. *Izvestiya,* January 14, 1979.

4. *Washington Post,* March 23 and May 10, 1979.

5. "Soviet Military Buildup," *Kyodo,* December 12, 1980, as reported in *Daily Report,* Foreign Broadcast Information Service, December 12, 1980 (hereafter cited as FBIS).

6. "Brezhnev Report on the 26th CPSU Congress," February 23, 1981, translated and reported by FBIS, February 23, 1981 (hereafter cited as "Brezhnev Report").

7. "Soviet Submarines Stationed in Malacca Strait," *Xinhua,* May 1, 1980, reported by FBIS, May 12, 1980.

8. "Brezhnev Report," FBIS, February 23, 1981.

9. *Xinhua,* January 20, 1980, reported by FBIS, January 21, 1980.

10. "Constitution of the Chinese Communist Party," *China Quarterly* 72 (1977): 918.

11. "Chairman Hua's Political Report," *Xinhua,* August 22, 1977, reported by FBIS, August 22, 1977. (Chairman Hua's report was delivered to the Eleventh National Congress of the Communist Party of China on August 12, 1977.)

12. Speech by Deng Xiaoping at the Chinese Communist Party's Third Plenary Session of the Tenth Central Committee on July 20, 1977 (hereafter cited as Deng's 1977 speech). For reference to this committee's meeting of July 21, 1977, see *Peking*

Review 20, no. 31(1977): 3-11.

13. "Joint Communiqué on the Establishment of Diplomatic Relations Between the United States of America and the People's Republic of China, December 15, 1978." See Hungdah Chiu, *China and the Taiwan Issue* (New York: Praeger, 1979), p. 225.

14. Deng's 1977 speech.

15. Ibid.

16. *Christian Science Monitor,* June 10, 1980.

17. FBIS, June 6, 1980. Four Chinese leaders—Wang Dongxing, Wu De, Ji Dengkui, and Chen Xilian—were expelled from the Politburo.

18. *Zhongguo Qingnian Bao,* January 17, 1981, as translated and reported in FBIS, January 30, 1981.

19. *Renmin Ribao,* February 28, 1981, as translated and reported by FBIS, March 10, 1981.

20. *Renmin Ribao,* January 26, 1981, as translated and reported by FBIS, February 9, 1981.

21. Franz Michael, *China Since Mao: A Travel Report,* Institute for Sino-Soviet Studies, reprint series no. 74, Fall 1978.

22. Yu Ch'iu Li [Yu Qiuli], "We Must Learn from Taiwan," *Inside China Mainland* (Taipei: Institute of Current China Studies), (December 1979) pp. 1-2.

23. *Asahi Shimbun,* March 12, 1981, as translated and reported in FBIS, March 13, 1981, annex.

24. *Gongren Ribao,* February 19, 1981, as translated and reported by FBIS, March 10, 1981.

25. The GNP figures were compiled by Herbert Block, economic consultant to the U.S. Department of State. The trade figures for all the noncommunist Asian ten, except Taiwan, are from the International Monetary Fund; Taiwan information is from U.S. Department of Commerce, January–November 1980.

2 | U.S. FOREIGN POLICY IN THE 1980s: SOUTH AND SOUTHWEST ASIA

*Walter K. Andersen**

For the second time in a decade the United States is assessing its policies toward the states of Asia. Soviet assertiveness, particularly in the Persian Gulf region, has aroused concern that the United States is militarily falling behind the USSR and that Moscow is gaining strategic advantages in critical areas. In response, the U.S. military budget has been increased, U.S. military forces in the northwest Indian Ocean have been strengthened, and an attempt has been made to build a strategic consensus among the United States and the regional states.

A key question is whether all this will impress the Soviets. The answer will depend on how military and foreign policy is implemented. Particularly important will be clearly stating U.S. interests and convincing the USSR and regional states that America is prepared to commit itself over time to the defense of these interests. Equally important for blunting Soviet strategic gains are increased self-confidence of Asian nations and better relations among the noncommunist states in the area.

From the Korean War to the early 1970s, U.S. policy rested on the concept of containing communism. The strategic objectives were to deter aggression and to meet force with force if deterrence failed. Public support for a comprehensive containment policy eroded in the wake of Vietnam,

---

*The views and opinions expressed here are those of the author and do not necessarily represent the policies or perceptions of the Department of State.

where there seemed no clear American interest to justify the enormous human and material costs. After the huge economic expenses of the Vietnam War and the demands generated by Johnson's Great Society, the American public would not permit the expenditures necessary to maintain the levels of military force needed to contain communism in both Europe and Asia. Indeed, the lesson that some drew from Vietnam was that the United States should totally disengage itself from Asia.

President Nixon responded to this pressure by fashioning a set of policies that envisaged greater reliance on regional allies for the burden of security and improved relations with the two communist giants. (The only country in Asia that fit the role of regional ally was Iran for the Persian Gulf.) Détente aroused the hope that a web of interrelationships with the USSR would restrain Soviet behavior.

The USSR insisted on an international managing role at least equivalent to that of the United States. Moscow was certainly not going to be contained when it perceived the United States withdrawing from an internationally activist stance. When the opportunity presented itself, the USSR sought to fill power vacuums around the world. The Soviet Union consequently continued to spend enormous sums on defense and to exploit regional instability to enhance Soviet influence at the expense of the West. The magnitude of Soviet military expenditures clearly signaled an intention to project Soviet power internationally.

Two events in the late 1970s undermined assumptions that had governed U.S. policy throughout the decade: the revolution in Iran and the Soviet occupation of Afghanistan. The former demonstrated that the United States could not rely on regional powers to protect Western access to critical energy resources and to limit Soviet influence. The latter shattered the illusion of Soviet restraint, particularly in the oil-rich Middle East.

The 1980s opened with the United States again formulating a policy to contain Soviet aggressiveness. The focus of American concern in Asia is the unstable area of southwest Asia extending from Turkey to India, which the British referred to as the "northern tier" and some in the United States later called the "arc of crisis." In this region, vulnerable to Soviet threats and pressure, the United States has suffered a number of strategic setbacks over the past decade. The Central Treaty Organization (CENTO), the containment vehicle of the "northern tier," collapsed in 1979. The Iranian revolution removed a regime supporting regional stability and replaced it with a successor that may try to export Islamic fundamentalism. Southern Asia was consigned to a diplomatic back burner.

For its part, the USSR has steadily strengthened its military presence in this region over the past two decades. The USSR gained its first access to the area during the early 1960s through a series of military aid agreements with Somalia. In March 1968, a Soviet flotilla sailed to the Indian Ocean from Vladivostok. This deployment began concurrently with the British decision to withdraw east of Suez; Moscow thus signaled its intention to play a role in the affairs of the area.

Since 1968, Moscow has maintained a continuous, though fluctuating, naval presence in the northwest Indian Ocean. In the mid-1970s the USSR developed Berbera (in Somalia) into its prime Indian Ocean support facility. The Ethiopian revolution provided Moscow still further opportunities for influence. Following their ouster from Somalia in 1977, the USSR turned to Ethiopia and received access to airfields there as well as in the People's Democratic Republic of Yemen. Air and naval facilities in Yemen provided staging bases for Soviet and Cuban military assistance to Ethiopia. In return for about $1.5 billion in military assistance between 1977 and 1980, the Ethiopians have permitted Moscow anchorage rights at the Red Sea island of Dahlak, thus providing interdiction capabilities to the Soviets at the choke point of the Red Sea through which Suez Canal traffic transits. In 1978, the aircraft carrier *Minsk* and an accompanying task force sailed into the Indian Ocean. The Soviets that same year received increased access to air and naval facilities in Yemen. The Soviet invasion of Afghanistan in late 1979 placed the USSR closer to the vital choke point of the Persian Gulf—the Strait of Hormuz; simultaneously the USSR upgraded its naval forces in the Indian Ocean.

Prior to the Afghan crisis, the United States maintained a smaller permanent presence, which used naval facilities at Bahrain in the Persian Gulf, through the 1970s, supplemented by periodic visits of naval task forces in the Indian Ocean. The presence of the U.S. task force became continuous in November 1978, and the United States (as well as the USSR) substantially increased deployments to the region as the crises in Iran and Afghanistan developed. In late 1980 the Western powers had approximately sixty warships in the western Indian Ocean, about one-half of which were American. The largest non-American contingent is French. France is presently the only Western state with troops stationed in the area, at Djibouti and Réunion, and is also the only Western power that permanently deploys air units to the region. French interests in the region fundamentally parallel those of the United States: political stability and Western access to petroleum resources.

The Soviets during the same period had 29 ships in the area. The United States has encouraged its NATO allies to do more to protect the oil-rich gulf area and has asked the Japanese to assume a greater role in defending the northwest Pacific region so that U.S. ships in the Pacific could be shifted to the Indian Ocean.

President Carter, in his 1980 State of the Union Address, declared that a goal of U.S. policy is to build a security framework in the region to protect our interests. He warned that "an attempt of any outside force to gain control of the Persian Gulf region will be regarded as an assault on the vital interests of the United States. It will be repelled by any means necessary, including military force."[1]

To back up this announcement, the president ordered the formation of a rapid deployment force, with its own permanent planning staff designed to respond quickly, even pre-emptively, to sudden threats arising in the gulf region. He also ordered an increased deployment of ships to the area. Because the effectiveness of a rapid deployment force depends on staging points and prepositioned supplies, stress was placed on acquiring access rights to naval and air facilities in Oman, Somalia, and Kenya. The United States also decided to upgrade the base at Diego Garcia to enable it to handle Strategic Air Command B-52s, C-5 transports, and aircraft carriers. In addition, plans were formulated for a new security relationship with Pakistan. The long-range goal of this program is the fashioning of a conventional force structure that can effectively deal with all contingencies short of a determined Soviet assault and that will, at the same time, make such an assault highly dangerous and hence less probable.

The Reagan administration, building on this foundation, significantly increased the military budget to provide the United States with the potential capability for projecting American power to the Persian Gulf without simultaneously reducing the strength of U.S. forces in the Pacific and in Europe.

There is little debate over the critical national interest in safeguarding Western access to the oil resources of the Middle East. In 1979, the Middle East was the source of some 21 million barrels per day of crude oil, about one-third the world total. The Persian Gulf states produce most of this crude oil, and 95 percent of the gulf oil is shipped through the Strait of Hormuz, the vital choke point of the gulf. The United States itself receives from the Persian Gulf states a relatively small part of its total oil imports—1.741 million barrels per day of 6.48 million barrels per day imported in 1979.[2] Western Europe and Japan, on the other hand, are heavily reliant on the Persian Gulf states for their crude oil requirements. The Federal Republic of Germany, for example, receives approximately one-half of its crude from the region. France, Italy, and Japan import about 70 percent of their unrefined petroleum from the Persian Gulf states.

Many analysts believe that the Soviet Union itself may soon become a major buyer of Persian Gulf oil. Although the USSR has large reserves of oil, the high extraction and transportation costs from the new Siberian fields will continue to make the nearby cheaply produced oil of the Persian

Gulf an attractive source. (In the Persian Gulf, for example, oil costs about $.45 per barrel to extract, while that in the new Siberian fields costs about $3 per barrel, which does not, of course, cover high transportation costs for the Siberian oil.) Moscow's Eastern European allies already purchase significant amounts of crude oil from the Persian Gulf states. Should the Soviets establish a pre-eminent managing role in the gulf and over the use of its resources, the world strategic balance would shift decisively in Moscow's direction.

The Soviets recognize that the West has interests in the Persian Gulf, as Brezhnev's comments to the Twenty-Sixth Congress of the Communist Party of the Soviet Union (CPSU) indicate. In his speech to the Congress, he stated that "by joint efforts and by taking the legitimate interests of all sides into account, it is possible to create in this region [the Persian Gulf] an atmosphere of stability and calm; it is possible to guarantee the sovereign rights of the region's states and security of sea and other communications lines linking it to the rest of the world."[3] But the USSR may not factor these interests into its strategic considerations if the West does not demonstrate the will and the means to protect its vital stake in the region.

So far, the USSR has continued to build up its military strength in the Horn of Africa and in the Soviet territory north of Iran and Afghanistan. In his discussion of Persian Gulf security, Brezhnev specifically excluded the Afghan domestic situation, which forces the Soviets to maintain large ground and air forces in Afghanistan.[4] The USSR knows that a Soviet client state there can exist only with the assistance of Soviet forces.

Any U.S. foreign policy would prove bankrupt, and potentially subject to wild fluctuations, unless Washington moves to redress the military balance with the USSR. A significant military buildup would go a long way to restore confidence abroad that we have the will and the discipline to maintain a solvent foreign policy. The experience of Soviet intervention in Europe and Asia suggests that the cautious Kremlin bureaucrats will act only after they have concluded that the United States will remain immobilized. When the Soviets occupied Hungary, Czechoslovakia, and Afghanistan, they knew that there was little chance of a Western military response. A credible response to the Soviet movement in southwest Asia, therefore, involves both a clear statement of U.S. intentions and a military buildup in the region.

A long-range check on Soviet assertiveness in Asia will fail unless the United States can sustain domestic political support for its policies after the initial shock of Afghanistan has faded from public memory, as well as strengthen the confidence and support of its allies. Both objectives will require considerable political dexterity. It is unclear if a new domestic foreign policy consensus has been established. Commitments must not extend beyond public support, and the use of military force must be tied to clear national interests. America's allies will be reluctant to make a substantial contribution to a broad strategy of blunting Soviet aggressiveness unless the United States demonstrates that it will do so on a sustained basis and unless the United States shapes its policies in close consultation with them.

The growing perception of threats to Western security has renewed the allies' sense of dependence on U.S. military might. But these perceptions do not necessarily translate into automatic allied support for American policies, particularly in the case of those U.S. initiatives that call for common alliance responses outside the NATO treaty area. There has been a growing tendency on both sides of the Atlantic to see world problems and their solutions in different terms. Despite European concerns about Soviet actions and intentions, Europeans and their governments continue to favor an effort to sustain a dialogue with Moscow, including arms control talks, along with moderate measures to meet Soviet expansionism to improve the arms balance. The USSR and its Warsaw Pact partners are not distant adversaries, but fellow inhabitants of the same continent. Repairing the ripped fabric of Europe is a deeply felt aspiration of the allied powers, especially the Federal Republic of Germany. The fact that Western Europeans would be on the firing line in the event of a major confrontation between the Soviet Union and the United States is a powerful inducement for them to reduce the chances of conflict.

Allied perceptions of the situation in southwest Asia do not coincide with those of the United States. Although the Afghan crisis has raised disturbing questions for them about Soviet global ambitions, they have not seen it as presenting a direct threat to their own security. Nor do they see it as part of a larger Soviet design to expand control in southwest Asia. The allies presently seem inclined to view the Afghan crisis as an east-south problem, and the initiatives for an international conference suggested by British Foreign Minister Peter Carrington and former French President Giscard d'Estaing are aimed at keeping the crisis from becoming an issue pitting East against West.

Generally, support for U.S. policies in the Middle East will be conditioned by the allies' conception of European concerns concentrated on an axis of international relations based on developed versus developing nations. Continued access to the region's oil is high on the list of concerns. Some of the European states have pursued independent policies in the hope of guaranteeing such access. In addition, the need to find new markets has assumed an increasing significance in view of stagnant economic growth, unemployment, and the need to finance ever more costly oil imports. Finally, some allies believe that a prudent political and economic response to Third World needs may prove a more effective counter to Moscow's influence than military response because it will help blunt the Soviet goal of aligning itself with the forces of change. The political demands of domestic European politics need not produce policies that contradict those of the United States, but Washington must consult closely with them so that the policies are complementary and, at a minimum, ensure that they are not at odds with each other.

The Soviets will surely try to diminish Europe's apprehensions about the motives of the USSR, without at the same time abandoning their longtime commitment of establishing a favorable correlation of forces that gives them a pre-eminent role in the management of Asian relations. The conservative Soviet leadership will be inclined to avoid a direct confrontation while Western concerns are aroused. In the interim, they can be expected to mount a diplomatic campaign aimed at halting Western military expansion. At the twenty-sixth CPSU congress in an appeal carefully crafted for Western audiences, Brezhnev proposed an "active dialogue" with the United States on disarmament issues. He also renewed Soviet calls for an international conference to discuss the Middle East. Earlier during his December 1980 trip to New Delhi, he raised the notion of a conference to discuss a Persian Gulf zone of peace.

These proposals, which all leave Soviet gains in the Horn of Africa and Afghanistan intact, are propaganda vehicles aimed at convincing Third World countries and our European allies—and perhaps a domestic U.S. audience as well—that the Soviet Union is reasonable and the United States is intransigent. Similar tactics were adopted at the 1981 meetings of the U.N. Ad Hoc Committee on the Indian Ocean, where the USSR actively backed a conference on the subject to be held during the summer of 1981 at Colombo. The Western powers unanimously opposed such a conference at that time on grounds that the Soviet military buildup on the Horn of Africa, in Afghanistan, and in the southern sectors of the USSR, not the Western naval response, constitutes the real threat to the littoral states.

The Soviet Union can support the zone of peace concept in the Indian Ocean since it does not need a navy to project its power to the Persian Gulf. It can project its power from the Caspian Sea, the Transcaucasus, and now from Afghanistan. Thus, the Soviets could inexpensively deny access to the Indian Ocean to the United States through an arms control agreement that does not cover the Soviet arms buildup to the north.

A parallel Soviet move would involve providing military assistance, economic aid, and diplomatic support to regimes that feel threatened by domestic dissidents and by unfriendly neighbors. Moscow has adroitly employed this approach along the periphery of the Persian Gulf—South Yemen, Ethiopia, and Syria—to enhance Soviet influence. This approach offers Moscow three advantages: distance from local controversies, the use of third parties to push Soviet interests, and a role in the resolution of local conflicts.

A related tactic is the support of subversion to place leftist pro-Soviet regimes in power. Iran is a likely target, but almost every country in southwest Asia is seething with unrest fueled by ethnicity, Islamic fundamentalism, and modernization.

These strategies underscore the fact that most Asian states look at a sharpened U.S.-Soviet confrontation largely in terms of the opportunities and dangers that such rivalry presents for their individual interests. A relatively powerful and stable state such as India vigorously advocates the withdrawal of all superpower forces from the Indian Ocean and its littoral. However, other Asian states tend to take a more ambiguous stand. Vietnam and South Yemen, for example, believe that closer links with a superpower will provide them with military protection as well as access to economic, technological, and diplomatic assistance. The perceived danger may be a superpower, the ally of a superpower, and some historic regional enemy. In addition, some seek assistance to strengthen central authority against various types of dissidents. These local interests both complicate and provide advantages to the USSR and to the United States. An American effort to wean Vietnam away from the USSR, for example, would be made enormously more difficult by Sino-Vietnamese competition for influence in Laos and Kampuchea. Similarly, U.S. efforts to build a security relationship with Pakistan could be undermined by a shift by India toward the USSR. Further, strengthening Western influence in Iraq could simultaneously drive the Iranians closer to the USSR. Alternately, Soviet assistance to Iraq would undermine Soviet efforts to rebuild a cordial relationship with Tehran. It is not difficult to understand why both the USSR and the United States have been studiously neutral on the Iran-Iraq war. The lesson to be drawn from all this is that the United States must be sensitive to the political, cultural, and strategic differences among the various Asian regions. Unlike Europe, Asia is too diverse for an integrated tactical approach.

U.S. policy in south Asia has vacillated widely since the withdrawal of the British from the region in 1947. Pakistan's hesitation about establishing a security relationship with the United States in 1980 underscores the regional perception of U.S. inconsistency. India's apprehensions that increased U.S. arms supplies to Pakistan might quickly blossom into a military alliance among China, the United States, and Pakistan are similarly colored by memories of America's roller-coaster policies in south Asia.

A succession of presidential administrations has shifted alternately between India or Pakistan, leaving a legacy of suspicions concerning U.S. intentions in both countries. As the cold war intensified in the 1950s, the United States was preoccupied with containing the USSR. The Eisenhower administration developed close relations with Pakistan, which provided the United States with intelligence-gathering facilities. During the Kennedy administration, U.S. efforts to contain China led to closer relations between India and the United States. Washington extended massive economic aid to India in the wake of the 1962 Sino-Indian war. The U.S. position shifted again as a result of the growing ties between Moscow and India, culminating in the 1971 Indo-Soviet Treaty of Friendship and Cooperation.

After the 1971 Indo-Pakistani war, south Asia became relatively unimportant as U.S. relations with China and the USSR improved. Washington's approach to New Delhi and Islamabad was governed more by global issues, such as nonproliferation of nuclear weapons and human rights, than by traditional balance-of-power concerns. The situation changed radically, however, with the Soviet's 1979 occupation of Afghanistan.

Pakistan's location—next to Afghanistan and Iran and close to the mouth of the Persian Gulf—makes its security an important element in any efforts to restrain the Soviets. A stronger, more self-confident Pakistan that is capable of resisting Soviet pressure through Afghanistan is in the interest of the United States. Indian support for efforts to remove Soviet troops from Afghanistan is similarly in the interest of the United States. Regional cooperation on the Afghan question would probably offer the best block to Soviet assertiveness eastward from Afghanistan. The USSR would be reluctant to take any action that threatens India's security interests since New Delhi is Moscow's major Asian counterweight to China. India possesses the world's third largest army, tenth largest industrial base, and third largest pool of technically trained workers. It has a large and sophisticated arms industry that produces all but the most advanced aircraft, warships, and tanks. It is one of the few politically stable states along the arc of crisis.

While India and Pakistan both consider the Soviet occupation of Afghanistan a destabilizing move and both want Soviet troops to leave, deep distrust between them inhibits cooperation. Periodic tensions have marred their relationship for three decades. The two states emerged in 1947 from British India in the midst of a breakdown of Hindu-Muslim communal relations throughout much of the northern areas of undivided British India. A war quickly broke out between the two states over the possession of Kashmir, where Muslims were in the majority. Pakistan demanded this former princely state of British India on the grounds that a contiguous area predominantly Muslim should go to a state that had been established as a homeland for the subcontinent's Muslim population. India regarded secession of Indian Kashmir as a violation of the secular principle on which India is based. As a result of that first war, Kashmir is now divided between India and Pakistan, and the division is still a source of tension.

Two subsequent wars have been fought between the two south Asian states. The last one in 1971 resulted in the secession of Bangladesh from Pakistan, and Pakistan fears that India would like further to balkanize it. India for its part believes that Pakistan wants revenge for past defeats and seeks outside military assistance to achieve this goal.

In addition, the two sides have no consensus regarding their security role in subcontinental affairs. India believes that its security, as well as that of the whole subcontinent, would be best safeguarded if it played a pre-eminent managing role. For this reason, New Delhi wants no outside power undermining this objective by establishing a security relationship with Pakistan. India would prefer that Pakistan assume the role of a strictly neutral buffer with a limited military potential. Such a state would not attract the attention of larger powers such as the USSR. Pakistan is unwilling to play this role and has historically looked for outside supporters unallied with India and, more recently, the USSR.

The major objective of Indian diplomacy in regard to Afghanistan is to insulate the subcontinent from the Afghan crisis and to remove it from a cold war context. With this in mind, the Indians publicly claim that the Soviet Union's intentions in Afghanistan are limited largely to shoring up a tottering regime on a strategic border, though Indian leaders probably do not expect the USSR to leave Afghanistan in the near future. The United States and Pakistan, on the other hand, view the Soviet action as creating new targets of opportunity for Moscow in neighboring regions. The USSR is now in a position both to exercise leverage on Pakistan by direct threats through Afghanistan and to provide assistance to those Baluchi- and Pashtu-speaking dissidents seeking greater autonomy and to political opponents to the martial law regime of General Zia ul-Haq.

The United States and Pakistan maintain that the crisis has international ramifications and thus requires an international solution, involving some kind of multilateral pressure on the USSR. Pakistan has turned to the Islamic Conference and the United Nations to establish a framework for negotiations among the interested parties, but these efforts have stalled due to the Soviets' refusal to participate in them. The United States has imposed a number of economic sanctions on the USSR and has also increased its levels of military force in the Indian Ocean. Pakistan seeks to strengthen its military capabilities to deter aggression against it.

Indian leaders argue that this "confrontational" approach will not get the Soviets out of Afghanistan and will probably delay their exit. They argue that the issue should be settled in a regional context, by which the Indians mean that Pakistan and Iran should resolve their differences with the Babrak Karmal regime through bilateral negotiations. The Karmal regime proposed such talks on May 14, 1980. In that May 14 formulation, Karmal called for bilateral talks with Iran and Pakistan and for guarantees from the

USSR and the United States of nonintervention as a prerequisite for Soviet troop withdrawal.

Although New Delhi has not commented officially on the Afghan proposals, India would probably welcome talks as a useful first step in defusing the crisis. Pakistan turned down Karmal's invitation (as did Iran) on grounds that the Islamic Conference at its January and May 1980 meetings advised member states to withhold diplomatic relations with Kabul until after Soviet troops had withdrawn. Moreover, accepting such bilateral negotiations would lend credibility to the Afghan (and the Soviet) contention that the insurgency survives because of outside assistance, chiefly from Pakistan.

The United States and Pakistan are now discussing Pakistani needs in consideration of the Soviet invasion of Afghanistan and the ongoing insurrection there. Islamabad is extremely cautious about establishing a security relationship with the United States. From Pakistan's perspective, the United States let it down on two prior occasions—during the 1965 and 1971 Indo-Pakistani wars, when both countries were members of CENTO. In light of this history, Pakistan left CENTO, joined the nonaligned movement, and looked to the Islamic nations of the Middle East for diplomatic and economic support. From the United States' standpoint, the unequivocal communist aggression that would justify implementation of the 1959 executive agreement between the United States and Pakistan has never taken place. (Neither the 1965 nor the 1971 Indo-Pakistani wars presented such a situation.)

In 1980, President Zia rejected a two-year $400 million military-economic package from the United States on grounds that the risks—increased tensions with the USSR, India, and Iran, for example—were not worth the uncertain benefits for the Pakistanis. A major uncertainty involved the reliability of a 1959 executive agreement pledging the United States to consult with Pakistan if it is attacked by a communist power. In addition, Pakistan was unsure if it was included in the Persian Gulf area that the United States had pledged to defend. Still another factor inducing caution was the potentially adverse reaction of domestic Islamic fundamentalists and leftists toward a strengthened Pakistani relationship with the United States. Finally, Pakistan did not want to undermine its credibility within the Islamic Conference and the nonaligned movement. These factors continue to condition the Pakistani response to a closer relationship with the United States, and it would be unwise for Washington to advocate a security relationship that a large part, if not the majority, of the Pakistani population would find unacceptable and that would create major bilateral problems with India, Iran, and the USSR.

Pakistan's dilemma is that all of its security choices are poor. There is uncertainty regarding the reliability and steadfastness of the United States. The Soviets cannot be trusted to honor a neutral Pakistan. Pakistan's Islamic allies are militarily weak. The Chinese may provide military assistance, but they are not likely to join Pakistan in a war with India or the USSR. Islamabad would be unwilling to bank on Indian guarantees of Pakistani security. Its new nonaligned credentials do not provide guarantees against outside aggression. Pakistan has neither the size, labor force, wealth, nor the industrial base to put together a credible defense against the USSR or India. With the collapse of CENTO and a less friendly regime in Tehran, it is now virtually surrounded by countries considered hostile or potentially hostile. Finally, Pakistan's strategic vulnerability is further compounded by its economic and political weakness as well as by the desire of its Baluchi-, Pashtu-, and Sindhi-speaking groups for greater autonomy.

The present Pakistani government, a military regime headed by Zia ul-Haq since 1977, has not gained legitimacy in the eyes of key social groups. However, as of mid-1981, he does not face a major threat to his position. The political opposition is divided and poorly organized. The economy is in relatively good shape. Zia has shown considerable skill in acting as broker among the various minority oppositions. The top military leaders seem satisfied with his handling of the government.

Nevertheless, a deterioration in the economy could lead to a quick coalescing of groups against Zia and his martial law government. Ethnic and religious tensions, now relatively quiescent, would under such circumstances become significant problems. There is no identifiable nonmilitary group ready to pick up the pieces, as the late President Ali Bhutto did in 1971. Consequently, a successor government would probably be another military figure lacking legitimacy.

U.S. and other Western economic assistance may improve the government's ability to satisfy the demands of important political groups and thus enhance its self-confidence. Greater assurance on the part of the military governors might induce them to broaden the presently narrow base of decision making. Military equipment would help Zia with his major constituency—the officer corps. However, reliance upon Pakistan as an anchor in any defense scheme for the Middle East seems dubious, given the fundamentally unstable nature of the Pakistani polity. Indeed, Pakistan itself would probably prefer that such a role not be thrust on it.

Pakistan for its part is likely to walk a tightrope, trying to keep problems with neighbors within manageable limits while cultivating outside supporters for security assistance and economic aid. Pakistan's outdated military equipment needs modern replacements, but Islamabad is not likely to accept a relationship of political and strategic dependency on the United States as the price of obtaining them.

In the interim Pakistan may seek economic assistance, and the Reagan administration in mid-1981 moved to reopen the economic aid pipeline. Pakistan may also seek to buy U.S. weapons on a straight cash basis at the best possible credit terms. The United States is considering a five-year military sales program at concessionary interest rates. Foreign Minister Agha Shahi visited the United States in April 1981 to discuss economic assistance and military sales. On his return to Pakistan, he told reporters that "in our talks with Washington we were able to agree on the principles which would govern a new bilateral relationship between the two countries, namely sovereign equality and respect for Pakistan's policy of non-alignment and its commitment to the positions taken by the Islamic Conference."[5] The key factor underlying the apparent change in the Pakistani position from 1980 seems to be greater confidence in the long-term reliability of the Reagan administration to pursue a consistent foreign policy. This development underscores the adverse consequences that rapid shifts of policy can have on the perception others have of the trustworthiness of the United States.

To provide economic assistance and military sales as well, the Reagan administration has sought to alter the 1977 Symington amendment to the Foreign Assistance Act of 1961, which prohibits certain types of economic and military assistance to countries that import uranium-processing technology, as Pakistan has done. The objective is to bring Symington in line with the Glenn amendment to the Foreign Assistance Act, which permits the president to provide military and economic assistance if he determines that a cutoff is prejudicial to U.S. security.

At the same time, the United States will surely continue to advise Pakistan against developing a nuclear explosive program. Although a nuclear deterrent seems particularly attractive for a smaller state against larger adversaries, such a program could actually undermine security; it might be both provocative and ineffective. India, already concerned about potential "erratic" behavior on the part of the Pakistani military leadership, would be even more concerned about Pakistani intentions. A Pakistani nuclear program would have a negative political impact in the United States as well and make it difficult to gain congressional approval for any economic or military assistance. Moreover, such a test would further undermine relations between India and the United States; New Delhi is likely to conclude that Washington acquiesced in a Pakistani testing program in the interest of a closer U.S.-Pakistani security relationship.

The considerable international publicity surrounding a Pakistani program to develop nuclear weapons has already aroused pressures in India to develop its own weapons program, which India could do much more quickly than could Pakistan. There is still considerable opposition in India to developing a nuclear weapon. This can be traced to Prime Minister Jawaharlal Nehru's idealistic view that India would never develop a weapon. However, there has already been considerable modification of this view. Prime Minister Lal Bahadur Shastri, who succeeded Nehru in 1964, stated that he could not forsake a nuclear option for all time. In 1974, his successor, Indira Gandhi, ordered a test explosion. On returning to power in 1980, she abandoned Prime Minister Morarji Desai's public stand that a Pakistani nuclear program was not a threat to India. During the April 1981 parliamentary debate on defense, Gandhi stated that a Pakistani bomb would have "grave and irreversible" consequences on the subcontinent and that India would "respond in an appropriate way to such a development."[6] The Janata Party of former Prime Minister Desai even advocated a "matching nuclear effort" if Pakistan continues to develop its nuclear program. Prominent Indian journalists and writers on strategy have urged a renewed testing program. This action-reaction syndrome could lead to testing on both sides and a sharp deterioration of bilateral relations.

Present U.S. policies focus on punishing those who proliferate. This approach has failed to influence nuclear programs in India and Pakistan because it did not adequately address the security concerns behind Indian and Pakistani nuclear aspirations. Rather, U.S. policies reinforced beliefs in both countries that Washington's policies were arbitrary and discriminatory. Finally, America overestimated its leverage on India and Pakistan.

Perhaps the only possible way for the United States to exercise some influence on the nuclear plans of the south Asia nations is to treat the nuclear issue as part of the security calculations of both India and Pakistan. One part of the U.S. effort should be to encourage Pakistan, India, and China to reconcile their disputes at the bargaining table. A south Asian program for negotiation of equivalent reduction in military forces might be still another step. In addition, the United States can help the various states fill in military deficiencies to improve defense capability. Nevertheless, India and Pakistan at the least will probably retain a nuclear option. During this decade, they will undoubtedly be in a position to put together a weapon. Neither is likely to give up that option, but efforts should continue to prevent either from exercising it.

The Indians recognize the potentially destabilizing consequences of the Soviet occupation of Afghanistan and have called on the USSR to withdraw its troops. New Delhi, however, faces the prospect of three possible outcomes to the Afghanistan crisis; as in the case of Pakistan, all are bad. The first is the continued occupation of Afghanistan by the USSR. A second is the emergency of an Islamic republic. Finally, there is the possibility of direct U.S. military involvement in the region.

U.S. assistance to Pakistan, in New Delhi's view, would begin to involve other countries in the rivalry between India and Pakistan, possibly endangering India's security. In addition, India believes that U.S. arms to Pakistan would adversely affect Indian security in two other ways. First, Pakistan's martial law regime would be less inclined to broaden the base of its support and thus would be more subject to domestic unrest and Soviet-inspired subversion. Both would undermine India's interest in a stable buffer between itself and Soviet troops in Afghanistan. Second, India believes that a militarily strengthened Pakistan will be less inclined to resolve its bilateral problems with India. A Pakistan fortified by sophisticated arms and a security guarantee from the United States might even be tempted to seize the disputed state of Kashmir. It is this apprehension that gives rise to the continually repeated Indian warning that American arms would ultimately be used against India, whatever the United States' intentions might be.

The intensity of distrust between these two Asian neighbors guarantees Indian opposition to any U.S. effort to strengthen Pakistan's security. India's response, however, might not necessarily undermine the United States' goal of blunting Soviet aggressiveness. Indian leaders already admit that Pakistan has legitimate defense concerns and have so far reacted with relative restraint to the news of possible U.S. military sales to Pakistan. If U.S. arms are geared to strengthening Pakistani military needs on its western border with Afghanistan and any future security guarantee is placed in the context of a Soviet threat, India will probably not take steps to neutralize America's effort to strengthen Pakistan. It is not in India's interest to weaken Pakistan's ability to defend itself against the USSR. Nor is it in India's interest to antagonize the United States. India wants to avoid a sharp deterioration of its relations with the United States since that would severely restrict its diplomatic maneuverability. Such a development could also have had an adverse effect on India's economy. The United States is India's largest trading partner and is a major source of its development funds; it also possesses the high technology that India seeks. Additionally, it is one of the few countries with sufficiently large amounts of exportable foodstuffs to satisfy Indian requirements in an emergency.

The United States might ameliorate India's suspicions of its intentions by making clear to New Delhi that Washington recognizes India's powerful role in Asia. Some possible approaches might include regular high-level political talks on the security situation in south and southwest Asia, offers to sell arms, and economic assistance. Simultaneous Chinese and Pakistani moves to improve bilateral relations with India should accompany any U.S. effort to strengthen Pakistan's security, to assure India that there is no emerging anti-Indian axis of the United States, China, and Pakistan.

However, there are divergencies in Indian and American policies regarding Soviet assertiveness in south and southwest Asia that are likely to create problems in bilateral relations through much of this decade. Besides India's opposition to the sale of U.S. arms to Pakistan, New Delhi is against the expansion of the American base at Diego Garcia, the U.S. naval buildup in the Indian Ocean, and U.S. access to naval and air facilities on the northwest Indian Ocean littoral on the grounds that these steps will only exacerbate the superpower conflict. It opposes an international solution to the Afghan question for the same reason. It advocates an Indian Ocean zone of peace conference. Although these differences will create tensions, it is in the interest of both sides to keep such differences within manageable limits since there are important economic and strategic reasons to maintain relations on an even keel. A determined Indian tilt toward the USSR would alter the balance of power in Asia, and the United States should shape its policies with a view to keeping India neutral.

The Chinese want to prevent India from drifting into the Soviet orbit. The decision in 1976 to exchange ambassadors after a fifteen-year hiatus underscored a marked reduction of Chinese suspicions of Indian intentions. To assure the Indians about China's desire for good relations, Chinese officials informed former Foreign Minister Atal Bihari Vajpayee during his visit to Beijing in 1979 that Chinese assistance to dissident tribals in northeast India was "a thing of the past." They have toned down criticism of Indian policy. They have suggested that India and China accept the present line of control as the boundary or at least put the contentious border dispute aside while the two sides strengthen the fabric of relations. There was a jolt when Gandhi, who returned to power in early 1980, recognized the Vietnamese-installed Heng Samrin regime in Kampuchea. The return visit of Foreign Minister Huang Hua to New Delhi was delayed as Beijing watched the development of Indian policy under Gandhi. China's decision to go ahead with the visit in June 1981 demonstrates that it believes that India has not lurched toward Moscow.

So far, the Chinese appear assured that New Delhi is not allying itself with Moscow. At the time of Brezhnev's December 1980 visit to New Delhi, the Chinese media blasted the USSR while giving the Indians high marks for keeping their distance from the various Soviet proposals. India was praised for its handling of the February nonaligned meeting in New Delhi. On April 8, 1981, Deng Xiaoping, according to Indian press reports, told Subramaniam Swamy, an Indian member of parliament, that "there should be an atmosphere of friendliness and spirit of mutual give and take" and that "there is no conflict of fundamental interests between China and India."[7] As long as New Delhi avoids a close strategic relationship with the USSR, it is in Beijing's interest to maintain amicable ties with a militarily strong neighbor that shares a long, common border. China, while supporting the rearmament of Pakistan, is likely to encourage Islamabad and Washington to keep their relations with New Delhi on an even keel.

India is delicately balanced between East and West, veering slightly one way or the other depending on the behavior of the superpowers. Should the Soviets become more aggressive toward Pakistan, for example, New Delhi may react by quickening the pace of rapprochement with China. The last time New Delhi seemed to be moving closer to Beijing, the Soviets were quite concerned and offered India a number of inducements to retain its friendship. Alternately, India can also be expected to veer somewhat closer to the USSR if the United States offers Pakistan excessive economic and military aid.

Afghanistan also presents a dilemma. The United States cannot acquiesce in the continued Soviet occupation of Afghanistan. Soviet troops are now within 300 miles of the Strait of Hormuz; the USSR is in a strengthened position to put pressure on Iran and Pakistan; a neutral state has been overwhelmed by a superpower. The Carter administration's policy was to convince the USSR that the costs of aggression outweigh the strategic gains, and this approach remains U.S. policy. It is unlikely, however, that any political efforts will get the Soviets out. A Soviet client regime would collapse immediately after the foreign troops left. Consequently, it will probably take consistent pressure on the USSR to underscore the point that it is in its interest to pull its troops out. However, such pressure should not provoke Moscow either to increase its troop commitment in Afghanistan or to engage in subversive activities in Pakistan and Iran. The struggle for freedom in Afghanistan demonstrates the massive resistance to Soviet political domination. Moscow will have to take this factor into consideration as it works out a long-term policy toward Afghanistan.

The United States has supported the notion of an international conference to resolve the crisis. The diplomatic task is to work out an international arrangement that prohibits outside involvement in Afghanistan's domestic affairs. Such an arrangement does not guarantee domestic stability. Indeed, there is likely to be considerable internal jostling before a workable system finally emerges. However, the prospects that the USSR would participate are dim, and Afghanistan is likely to be a source of U.S.-Soviet tension throughout the 1980s.

The focus of American and Soviet competition in the 1980s will probably continue to be the arc of crisis region. Elsewhere in Asia, relatively stable state systems have emerged over the past two decades. In contrast, this region is rife with unresolved intraregional conflicts and unstable governments. The Arab-Israeli conflict and the Iran-Iraq fighting are likely to drag on for years. With the collapse of a strong central authority in Iran, the region around the Persian Gulf lost a stable security framework. With the exception of Israel, every nation faces the prospect of revolutionary attacks on the existing political order over the next decade.

The USSR wants to play a significant role in managing the resolution of these conflicts. It will exploit political instability to enhance its influence at the expense of the West. The physical proximity of the USSR and the massive military forces at its disposal provide Moscow with the leverage to exert pressure in the region and the means to intervene directly if it decides to do so. The only credible deterrents to a direct Soviet move are U.S. forces in the area. The United States must maintain a powerful naval presence in the northwest Indian Ocean to buy time for a resolution of the Palestinian question, to build a structure of security cooperation between America and the regional states, to strengthen the presently skeletal regional armies, and to build up the rapid deployment force.

The United States needs to develop a closer military relationship with the states in the area to make the rapid deployment force credible. Presently, the United States has a base at Diego Garcia in the middle of the Indian Ocean and access to Bahrain. Since the Afghan crisis, the United States has acquired access rights in Oman, Kenya, and Somalia. The Egyptians are also prepared to offer access rights to the planned air and naval base at Ras Banas.

Bases in the area would enable the United States to operate much more efficiently to counter a Soviet thrust. Firepower and troop size can be more modest if they are readily available for any contingency. Troops on hand can respond more quickly to the often ambiguous signals of hostility. However, none of the regional states are presently willing to grant the United States rights to bases, in large part because they fear being labeled United States clients by other Islamic states. They also fear that a visibly public association with the United States will give domestic leftists and anti-Western Islamic fundamentalists an opening to discredit their governments. These states want, in the words of some strategists, "a full U.S. presence, but one that cannot be touched."

The reluctance of regional states to grant basing rights is also conditioned by doubts concerning America's reliability in the face of a crisis. They were shaken by the appearance of vacillation at the time of the Shah's flight from Iran, as well as by the aborted attempt to rescue the U.S. embassy hostages. They will watch closely for any further signs of vacillation when another crisis develops.

Given these political constraints, the United States will probably have to keep a continuous troop presence near the Persian Gulf. These troops would need marines to defend air and naval bases that the rapid deployment force would use if fighting broke out.

The United States should immediately begin to lay the groundwork for an improved military relationship to draw the regional states into a closer security alignment with Washington. This strategy aims at building confidence among America's allies in the region. Simultaneously, a forthcoming response to requests for military assistance would underscore the United States' concern for the security of the regional states. This assistance should be followed by joint strategic planning and, finally, joint exercises.

A parallel effort to strengthen cooperation in regional security is the Persian Gulf Council for Cooperation, formed in 1981, which includes all peninsular states except the two Yemens. Such forums build up the habit of cooperation. However, the regional military forces are much too weak to handle any frontal Soviet attack, or even the assault of a regional Soviet surrogate. A powerful U.S. military presence is an essential complement to any regional military efforts. Moreover, the first meeting of the Persian Gulf Council in Muscat underscored the lack of consensus regarding the intensity of the Soviet threat or the necesssary response to it.

Finally, a willingness on the part of ruling elites to share power with newly politicized groups would probably do as much to insulate regional regimes from subversion and Soviet blandishment as any military security program. Further, forces of change are growing throughout the region, and the United States must not be perceived as the defender of a political order discredited by large parts of the population. Consequently, a certain distance from specific regimes is necessary to reduce the chances of the United States becoming too closely identified with them. As a practical measure, bases would give an undesirable appearance of closeness. Such bases would also damage the standing of regimes domestically and regionally.

A factor limiting U.S. security efforts in the Middle East is Israel's concern that U.S. arms shipments to Arab states endanger Israeli security. The chances of ameliorating Israel's concerns would be considerably improved if the Camp David peace talks succeed. It will take political dexterity to balance Israeli concerns with American efforts to strengthen the gulf states against a Soviet lurch southward.

The United States should leave no doubt that its forces in the area will be used in the event of a Soviet attack. Past history of Soviet action suggests that this will be sufficient to deter a frontal assault. However, there is still the question of revolutions or coups d'etat that bring to power leftist pro-Soviet regimes or anti-Western Islamic governments, both of which could endanger Western access to oil. This possibility also raises the issue of external assistance to such movements. South Yemen, for example, which is rapidly becoming a Soviet surrogate, actively assists the Popular Front for the Liberation of Oman and the National Democratic Front in the Yemen Arab Republic. Similarly, Iran might support Islamic fundamentalist groups that appear to be gaining increasing popular support.

Security for the United States demands that the oil continues to flow and that sea-lanes are protected. Such protection will be extremely difficult given the task of guarding the thousands of miles of oil pipeline that lace the area. That task is difficult even with a friendly regime in power and would be almost impossible with an unfriendly government determined to deny oil to the United States. A prudent response would be to support the existing generally pro-Western regimes of the region and to encourage them to develop a set of cooperative relations with each other. The experience of the past decade is a reminder that whoever controls the production of oil can interrupt production not only for economic ends but for political ends as well. Control of a larger fraction of the oil by a radical state could be much worse. Soviet control over the oil resources would be incomparably worse.

The 1980s will witness an increasing globalization of what had been Asian security issues. The Sino-Soviet competition in east Asia, the Sino-Vietnamese conflict in Southeast Asia, Indo-Pakistani tensions, as well as the various conflicts along the arc of crisis, increasingly affect U.S.-Soviet relations. This development means that U.S.-Soviet competition will to a large extent be mediated through regional tensions.

A policy of limiting Soviet aggressiveness faces a very different global power situation from that which existed in the 1950s and 1960s. The Soviet Union is militarily much stronger now. Our European allies are much more economically powerful and self-confident and thus more prepared to pursue their own foreign policy interests. The Third World presents a much more complex picture than it did earlier.

The development of common foreign policies on the part of our friends and allies will be limited by different perceptions of threat, divergent interests, and different national outlooks. American exhortations for allied solidarity may succeed in the context of a genuine exchange of views and the development of complementary policy approaches. Regional cooperation, certainly in south and southwest Asia, will reduce the chances of successful Soviet intervention and pressure.

The key factor in any effort to contain Soviet aggressiveness will be domestic American politics. The public must be willing to make and sustain the sacrifices to support a larger military budget as well as economic assistance. Prolonged economic sluggishness would undermine support both for a larger military establishment and for other types of overseas commitments. Another problem will be the popular demand for quick results. The task of political leadership will be to sustain support for blunting

Soviet aggressiveness without arousing false expectations of immediate solutions. Finally, bipartisan support on a general foreign policy and close cooperation between the executive and legislative branches are essential to reduce chances of policy reversals after each election of a new president or members of Congress. No sustained and consistent approach can exist without a broad popular consensus on the major foreign policy questions facing the country.

Notes

1. President Jimmy Carter, "State of the Union Address" (speech delivered to the U.S. Congress, Washington, D.C., January 21, 1980).

2. *International Energy Statistical Review* (Springfield, Va.: National Technical Information Center, 1980).

3. Leonid Brezhnev, speech delivered to the Twenty-Sixth Congress of the Communist Party of the Soviet Union, Moscow, February 23, 1981. Foreign Broadcast Information Service (FBIS), vol. 3, no. 036, supp. 001, p. 16.

4. Ibid., p. 20. At the congress, Brezhnev avoided the question of Soviet troops in Afghanistan: "We do not object to the questions connected with Afghanistan being discussed in conjunction with the questions of security in the Persian Gulf. Naturally here only the international aspects of the Afghan problems can be discussed, *not internal Afghan affairs*. The sovereignty of Afghanistan must be fully protected, as must its nonaligned status" (italics added).

5. Michael Fathers, dispatch in *Reuters,* Islamabad, May 2, 1981.

6. Indira Gandhi made this comment during a debate on April 8, 1981, in the Lok Sabha, India's lower house of parliament. FBIS, vol. 8, no. 69, p. El.

7. Deng Xiaoping made this comment to Subramaniam Swamy, an opposition member of India's parliament, during Swamy's visit to China. The Chinese have often used Swamy to convey some important message to India. For a report of his meeting with Deng Xiaoping, see *The Hindu* (Madras), April 11, 1981.

3 | U.S. POLICY IN ASIA: THE INDIA FACTOR

Leo E. Rose

The primary focus of this chapter on U.S. policy in south Asia is on the role of India in American policy perspectives and planning, both within the region and on a broader scale in southern Asia in general. Before we plunge into the murky depths of U.S. involvement in regional and subregional international developments in south Asia, however, a few comments on the general principles of American foreign policy, as these have been applied to the subcontinent, are appropriate. These principles not only appear to be well entrenched in Washington but also still determine to some extent the responses in New Delhi to American involvement in the region.

In 1975, Baldev Raj Nayar expressed an almost classic if somewhat outdated Indian perspective on relations between India and the United States; he emphasized the allegedly "anti-Indian" facets of American policy in the region and throughout Asia.[1] Nayar, an Indian scholar who has spent most of his long academic career in the United States and Canada, makes a reasonable analysis of the impact of American involvement in southern Asia on India, but demonstrates a consistent incapacity to comprehend even the basic policy objectives and motivations that underlie U.S. policy in the region. But this lack of comprehension has been a characteristic of much of Indian scholarship on the subject, particularly of the older group that was socialized into international politics in the 1950s. Although in some cases this reflects bias against the United States, far more often it is indicative of confusion—the result all too frequently of widespread misinformation emanating from American sources on U.S. foreign policy.

But it is more than that. Probably the principal reason for this confusion is that there have been no general principles underlying U.S. policy in Asia readily perceptible to the interested outsider, including Indians, since World War II. Instead, there has been a series of ad hoc decisions, narrowly defined to meet specific events and developments that were viewed as threatening to American interests and usually made outside of anything that can be defined as a broader policy framework. The containment policies of the 1950s and 1960s in southern Asia were, of course, an extension of foreign and strategic policies adopted in Europe and the Mediterranean, but lacked an integral and cohesive conceptual character. As defined for Asia, containment was exclusively a reactive policy in which the initiative by definition, and in contrast to our containment policy in Europe, was left to others. It was, in fact, a convenient device for limiting unwanted but unavoidable security commitments in Asia, but its usefulness depended in large part upon a policy of forbearance—or more precisely, the lack of capability to act effectively—by the major rivals of the United States in Asia.

It is hard to know who has been more confused and bewildered by the incoherence in U.S. policy in Asia—the U.S. government and public, our allies and friends, the so-called nonaligned powers, or our enemies. In such circumstances, it was not surprising that most Indian officials, academics, and journalists consistently misinterpreted the objectives of American policy in Asia and responded on numerous occasions in ways that made little sense even in terms of their perceptions of India's interests and needs. Global factors make flexibility a necessary ingredient in all U.S. policy decisions, and a rigorously and narrowly defined coherent policy for Asia is not feasible. But a broader degree of consistency in both identifying U.S. objectives and in correlating policy decisions in various parts of Asia would not only be helpful to the decision makers in Washington but also reassuring to the various Asian states, including India, that would prefer a greater degree of predictability in Washington's responses than has been the case in the past.

Nayar may have some problems in understanding the motivations behind American foreign policy, but his demand that India "be taken seriously" should be taken seriously. Still deeply entrenched in some official government circles is the proclivity to dismiss India as an irritant that can occasionally complicate decisions about Asian issues but that can be ignored or shunted aside at little cost to the efficacy of U.S. policies. Even more unfortunate, perhaps, is the lack of consideration given to the complementarity of U.S. and Indian interests on some critical issues—the withdrawal of Soviet forces from Afghanistan or the "neutralization" of Southeast Asia, for example—and the little effort expended in trying to devise ways in which the two governments can work together discreetly to achieve common objectives. More typically, the two governments have tended to criticize each other over what are at times minor differences in their approaches to the resolution of shared problems rather than attempt to work together to supplement each other's efforts. The limited cooperation between Washington and New Delhi on Soviet intervention in Afghanistan is merely the latest of several examples in which both sides preferred to accent the negative rather than seek the positive.

Why should the United States take India seriously? The arguments given usually refer to its size (700 million people) and its status as the world's largest democracy, sharing basic political and systemic values with the United States. These facts are certainly important, but not infrequently the Americans who argue—quite correctly—that China's huge population makes it dangerous to ignore are the first to dismiss India as an insignificant factor in Asian and world geopolitics. And, as is quite clear, shared values do not necessarily lead to a perception of shared interests, at least in short-range terms. There are, however, other factors that are important determinants of India's status and capacities in Asia, which do affect U.S. policies and deserve consideration.

First, and perhaps of most importance, India is the major economic and military power in southern Asia, and its status as such is likely to be considerably enhanced over the next two decades. It is not a dominant power; indeed, it is dependent on access to resources from other countries in the area and beyond to a considerable extent and will be for some years to come. But India's economic interaction through joint ventures with its neighbors throughout southern Asia has been growing rapidly over the past decade and will increase substantially in the future. And with a military force of a million men, including a growing navy and air force, India is the strongest regional military power in the Indian Ocean area; it is capable of acting beyond its territorial borders in certain situations. Thus India is likely to play an increasingly vital role in economic and security issues in southern Asia and must be treated accordingly.

Another basic fact of life is that any security system supported by the United States for southern Asia (or its subregions) would find opposition by India an almost insurmountable barrier. At the minimum, neutralization of India is essential to the construction of a security system that would both deter the Soviets and the Vietnamese from further expansionist policies and provide the state systems in the region with a greater sense of confidence in their own capacities to meet both external and internal challenges. Although direct Indian participation in such a security system may be highly unlikely (until and unless the Soviet threat to the subcontinent becomes so obvious that even New Delhi must adjust policy), some forms of tacit

Indian cooperation with such a system are now possible. But the situation demands a perspective in Washington that has been virtually nonexistent for the past decade, particularly under the Carter administration. Support for a regular system of consultation between the two governments above and beyond the ambassadorial level is needed. In the past, such consultations have usually occurred in the context of some crisis, either in the region or in relations between the two countries, and in most cases within conceptual and substantive frameworks so narrow that they limit discussions to the immediate issue at stake. The result, typically, was an exchange of views but no real effort to reconcile their positions.

One other factor that should enhance New Delhi's importance to American decision makers on a broad range of international issues is the central role of India in Third World and developing nations' organizations—the nonalignment movement and the group of 77, for example. India is particularly active in the formulation of policy positions on both political and economic international issues. Indians no longer dominate the process of preparing position papers for developing nations in current meetings between developed and developing countries as they once did, but they are still probably the single most important influence in defining the positions of countries in the developing worlds, excluding the Organization of Petroleum Exporting Countries (OPEC). The evident failure of several international conferences to reach anything more than pro forma agreements on a new international economic order that do not address the principal issues in dispute makes it incumbent upon the American government to enter intensive bilateral discussions on these subjects with the critical states in the south to work out acceptable compromises that are realistic and can be sold on a broader international basis. Certainly, India is one of the four or five governments that should be included in this process of negotiations, and periodic consultations between Washington and New Delhi could well contribute to the resolution of some of these problems or, even more important perhaps, encourage India to take a more critical position in regard to OPEC's policies toward other poor developing countries. In any case, it is ludicrous that India and the Soviet Union have established procedures for the discussion of international economic issues while the United States, which is far more important to India on such matters, has not. This oversight, politically at least, is at America's expense as well.

Although India's leadership in the nonalignment movement may have deteriorated considerably over the past decade, as was clearly demonstrated in the meetings in Havana in October 1979 and in New Delhi in February 1981, it still plays a critical and, in some situations, decisive role in the movement. In a novel approach, New Delhi has expanded its definition of nonalignment to include a nonaligned role for itself in the nonalignment movement, somewhere between the minority group led by Cuba, which seeks to align the movement with the Soviet bloc, and the truly nonaligned majority. In the 1981 meetings in New Delhi, India played an effective mediatory role that earned it the reputation of being as anti-Soviet as Singapore and reportedly distressed the Cubans and Soviets. The American government should provide whatever support it can to the truly nonaligned group in the nonalignment movement, but some encouragement should also be given to India to maintain its nonaligned role in the movement, even though this may be less than ideal from Washington's perspective. This is another instance in which limited accommodations between the United States and India, in which both sides accept their differences as well as their areas of agreement, might well improve American relations (that have ranged from the indifferent to the dismal) with an important group of developing countries.

The principal points I have sought to make here are: (1) that India is important to the United States in a variety of ways; (2) that there are significant areas of both shared and disparate interests between them; and (3) that it would be helpful to both governments if they could, for a change, stress the former rather than the latter interests. In the following sections of this chapter, I shall discuss why and how I consider this cooperation possible on several issues that have complicated interactions between the two states in the past, often for good reasons, but on which perceptions on both sides have been modified more recently by a series of traumatic developments.

The United States and India: Some General Issues

Since at least the mid-1960s, the one general principle underlying American policy in south Asia that has been noted by most commentators is that the region is peripheral to vital American interests and of importance primarily in terms of its impact on development in adjacent areas of southwestern or Southeast Asia. The southern Asian security systems introduced in the 1950s and the intervention in Indochina in the 1960s were primarily motivated by objectives external to south Asia—the containment of China in Southeast Asia and of the Soviet Union in southwest Asia. Pakistan and India were factors in both of these security systems, though in quite different ways, and this made some U.S. involvement unavoidable. But south Asian factors were generally ignored by the decision makers in Washington who found the tenaciousness demonstrated by both Indians and Pakistanis irksome and counterproductive because they concentrated on their own troubled relationship rather than on the more critical concerns as perceived by Americans.

It was with a sense of relief that the United States virtually opted out of any significant involvement in south Asia following the 1965 Indo-Pakistani war and no longer sought to challenge Moscow in its determined effort to expand Soviet influence throughout south Asia. On balance, of course, these developments had a negative impact on American relations with the south Asian states until the Soviet military intervention in Afghanistan and political chaos in Iran made it essential for both India and Pakistan to reconsider their basically negative attitude toward the American role in the subcontinent. There are, however, certain aspects of American policy positions on more general issues in Asia under the Carter administration that seriously complicated the efforts by both Islamabad and New Delhi to expand and improve relations with Washington, and there is still a good deal of uncertainty in both countries on the policy positions of the Reagan administration. We shall briefly examine some of these issues before turning to the more specific problems facing Washington in its relations with India.

The United States and China's Military Modernization

The debate in the United States over the potential American contribution to the modernization of China's military forces has focused almost exclusively on the Sino-Soviet military confrontation and its impact upon the European front. Although few Americans seriously argue that the United States can significantly alter the Chinese-Soviet military balance through a military aid program to China, the political implications of such a program on Chinese foreign and security policies and upon Beijing's relations with Washington are still the focus of discussion. U.S. officials and security and foreign area specialists continue to talk on this subject with little concern, or even notice, of the views expressed in India and other southern Asian states on an American military aid program to China. Rather typical is an article by Jonathan Pollack of the Rand Corporation that focused on the international implications of an arms aid program to China but never mentioned India.[2]

While Vietnam and its two client regimes in Indochina may be the only states in southern Asia that perceive China as an immediate military threat, Pakistan is probably the only one that demonstrates any enthusiasm over China's military modernization program. All the other states, including India, would interpret a large-scale American military assistance program to China, either in sophisticated equipment or in military-related and nuclear technology, as part of a de facto U.S.-China alliance system. Such an alliance would raise serious questions for their political and security policies, both national and regional. Although the responsible authorities in New Delhi are reasonably complacent about the current military balance between India and China, given Beijing's current security priorities, from past experience they realize that the situation can change drastically almost overnight because of the basic instability of the Chinese political system. A major military modernization program in China focused on the development of nuclear weapons and delivery systems—particularly if assisted by high-grade U.S. technological assistance to Beijing—would be a potent argument to already powerful political forces in India that advocate greater emphasis on a military modernization program of their own, including the actual production of nuclear weapons. The consequences for U.S. policy interests would be most serious because a likely side effect would be major Indian concessions on its Afghanistan and Pakistan-Iran policies to the advantage of the Soviet Union. Such actions would further complicate India's efforts to create a regional response to all forms of external intervention in southern Asia.

For several years now, India and China have been involved in a series of delicate negotiations and maneuvers intended to provide the basis for a substantial expansion and improvement in their relationship. There have been several irritating setbacks—the Chinese invasion of Vietnam in early 1979 and India's recognition of the puppet Heng Samrin government in Kampuchea in mid-1980, for instance—but after each instance the efforts have been renewed by both sides. Although there is probably little that Washington can do directly to influence those negotiations, it could indirectly affect them through its ties with Beijing. Because improved Sino-Indian relations are in the interest of the United States—as well as of China and India—and would be viewed with considerable distress by the Soviet Union, Washington should exercise great care in defining its policies toward China to avoid complicating matters for Beijing and New Delhi. In particular, New Delhi should be routinely informed about U.S. technological transfers to China and reassured that these do not threaten Indian security. Since the present Chinese government has placed top priority on economic modernization and a low priority on military modernization, public statements emanating from Washington should make the limits on U.S.-China cooperation in the military sphere clear to all interested powers, including the Soviet Union. In other words, the United States will not provide sophisticated equipment or technology that is primarily military in use but will rather encourage Beijing to retain the emphasis on economic modernization.

The Indian Ocean as a "Zone of Peace"

It has become an annual feature of the U.N. General Assembly to reaffirm by a nearly unanimous vote the resolution first adopted in 1971 calling for the declaration of the Indian Ocean as a "zone of peace." From this vote, one might assume overwhelming support for the concept of a total withdrawal of the military forces of the nonlittoral states from the Indian Ocean, but one would be wrong. Indeed, quite the opposite is the case. The support given to the proposition by the Soviet Union and its bloc of states is patently fraudulent, as was evident in 1977 when the Carter administration unexpectedly proposed serious negotiations with Moscow on this subject. But it is also now clear that most of the littoral states support the zone of peace proposal only conditionally and that such conditions do not exist currently and are not likely to do so in the foreseeable future. Indeed, the entire scenario on this issue in the United Nations is an incredible farce in which most of the governments of states bordering on the Indian Ocean feel free to support the zone of peace resolution precisely because it lacks credibility. If there were any chance that the principle might become operative, it is probable that most of the littoral states would do whatever was needed to make it unnecessary for them to express their position publicly. And according to some reports, there are so many reservations among these states in the context of the present situation in both Southeast and southwest Asia that the usual reaffirmation resolution may not even be introduced in the General Assembly for some time to come.

The United States continues to ignore the bizarre situation in which friendly states regarded as allies vote for the U.N. resolutions on the Indian Ocean—resolutions also supported by the U.S. vote in the General Assembly—and quietly inform the American government that their U.N. votes do not reflect their true position on the issue. Early in 1977, the Carter administration appeared to be ready to adjust U.S. policy in accordance with the U.N. resolution, apparently on the misunderstanding (1) that this is what the littoral states really wanted and (2) that a mutual withdrawal or limitation of Soviet and American military forces in the Indian Ocean involved an equal sacrifice in geostrategic terms by the two superpowers. Subsequent developments in U.S.-Soviet relations, the Iranian revolution and seizure of American hostages, the Afghanistan crisis culminating in direct Soviet military intervention in that country, and the Iran-Iraq war compelled Carter to reverse U.S. policy and move instead toward a much expanded military presence in the Indian Ocean and adjacent regions.

Most of the confusion in Washington on this issue, including within congressional circles, has dissipated but there are still occasions when political or government leaders appear to take the zone of peace proposal seriously. Several factors should be noted in this respect. First, both U.S. and Soviet commitments and interests in the Indian Ocean make a complete withdrawal of their respective naval and supportive forces implausible. The most that might be accomplished is an agreement limiting the superpowers' military forces and commitments in the southern Asia area, but this cannot be restricted to sea-based forces or limited to one section of the Indian Ocean. Brezhnev's proposal in New Delhi in December 1980 for a zone of peace in the Persian Gulf might provide the bare basis for beginning negotiations but nothing more. As proposed it only affects American military commitments in the Persian Gulf; to even deserve consideration the discussions must be extended to include Soviet facilities in the Red Sea provided by Ethiopia and South Yemen as well as the new Soviet airfields in Afghanistan. It must be re-emphasized to Moscow that the linkage principle does apply to Soviet and American involvement in southern Asia as a whole, including Afghanistan and southwest Asia, and that no settlement on military forces that is restricted to the Indian Ocean will be considered by the U.S. government. On the other hand, linkage of a reduced American military commitment to the Indian Ocean in exchange for a Soviet withdrawal from Afghanistan—that is, a return to the situation before December 1979—at least deserves consideration by Washington.

Second, with regard to the current differences between the United States and most governments of the littoral states over the greatly expanded American military presence in the Indian Ocean, note that the subject in dispute is not the United States' commitment but its terms and limitations. These governments are uncertain about American intentions and objectives, since these have not been spelled out clearly yet. Some suspect that this expansion may well be another loudly trumpeted but temporary commitment to the area that will be abandoned when it no longer serves U.S. convenience or interests, an aspect of U.S. policy in Asia that many of them have experienced in the past at a high cost to themselves. The establishment of another naval fleet on permanent assignment in the Indian Ocean would certainly go a long way to remove the uncertainty over long-term U.S. intentions and would probably reduce the hesitation with which several states in southwest Asia respond to American proposals for cooperation on security issues. India and some other littoral states would object—only as a formality—but it would be a sufficient response to note that all that the United States is doing is what the Soviet Union has done, with only rare public criticism, since 1968. The United States should, indeed must, insist upon equal treatment with the USSR on this issue in both the public and private positions of these governments and state clearly the inconsistencies in their public statements when these occur.

India has been the only littoral country in the region supportive of an immediate imposition of the zone of peace principles in the Indian Ocean, and recent developments have even raised some doubts on this question in New Delhi. Government sources still speak in ultimate terms on the issue, at least in public, but there is some evidence of a greater willingness to proceed more slowly today than in the past. India wants to see a trend of developments initiated that would eventually lead to the total withdrawal—or at least strict limitations—upon both U.S. and Soviet naval and military forces in the Indian Ocean. But I have the impression that it is now understood in New Delhi that the immediate achievement of this goal could undermine India's far more important diplomatic efforts to create a situation under which the Soviets might be persuaded to withdraw their military forces from Afghanistan, as well as to keep open India's access to vital oil resources through the Strait of Hormuz. Both require an American military presence in the Indian Ocean if only as a crucial bargaining chip in any future negotiations in which New Delhi will want to play a mediatory role.

The United States must clearly inform India that it will not even consider a reduction, much less a withdrawal, of the present American military commitment in the Indian Ocean except in the context of an agreement with the Soviet Union that encompasses both the ocean and southwest Asia, including Afghanistan, and not just the Persian Gulf. At the same time, however, Washington should impress upon New Delhi that it is open to a wide range of proposals on security issues in the region that neither places the United States at a distinct disadvantage nor endangers the security of friendly countries in the region. The government of India may just throw up its hands in total frustration in response, but it is also possible that it would try to evolve a more balanced policy of its own to achieve at least those objectives that serve both Indian and American interests.

Nuclear Nonproliferation Policy

Introduced in a pro forma manner in the late 1960s but not pressed with any enthusiasm until the Carter administration, U.S. policies directed at preventing the proliferation of nuclear weapons have been a failure. Although the number of openly acknowledged members of the "nuclear club" did not increase in the 1970s, this was more the result of self-restraint by nations close to developing nuclear power than a response to American pressure, denunciations, and punishments. The nonproliferation act—passed by Congress in 1978 and accepted by the administration—that defined retaliatory measures to be imposed upon those states that do not conform to American principles of acceptable behavior on the nuclear question is not only an arrogant piece of legislation but also one of the more ineffectual. Such a law might have had some capacity to influence decisions about nuclear weapons (except by the Soviet Union and China, of course) in the 1950s—when the United States was encouraging such countries as India to develop nuclear energy systems—but by the late 1970s it was much too late to use such pressure tactics to any effect. Indeed, it is probable that the policies imposed on the U.S. government by the 1978 legislation have been counterproductive by enhancing the security apprehensions of several countries interested in developing nuclear power. It is particularly ludicrous that under this law the United States can provide advanced technological assistance to China's nuclear program because China is already a nuclear power, but is barred from counterbalancing this in any way by maintaining existing assistance programs in countries such as India that feel threatened by China's nuclear weapons system.

The negative consequences of the 1978 legislation are probably best demonstrated in the act's impact on the 1963 agreement with India by which the United States provided nuclear fuel for the Tarapur nuclear power plant. Under the terms of this agreement between the two countries, Tarapur would remove what have been, according to American reports, effective international controls over the sources of plutonium available in the plant's storage facilities for the production of nuclear weapons if New Delhi should so decide. How this contributes to the American policy discouraging nuclear proliferation has never been explained, and indeed cannot be.

Nonproliferation is a sensible and reasonable objective, particularly if it can be combined with agreements that limit or, preferably, reduce the weapon systems of the nuclear powers. But an intelligent American policy can no longer be based upon the assumption that proliferation can be prevented through such prohibitive policies as the Nuclear Nonproliferation Treaty or the 1978 act. Instead, the U.S. government should focus on efforts to improve the security environment, which now appears so threatening to some nearly-nuclear powers that they are seriously considering the production of nuclear weapons and the necessary delivery systems that go with such weapons. Public reassurances that the United States will not assist China's nuclear program, for instance, would at least reduce the pressures upon India, Taiwan, and perhaps even South Korea in this respect. There could also be a favorable fallout (to use the term metaphorically) on other governments; Pakistan's nuclear program, for instance, is primarily a response to that of India, and it is possible that Islamabad would be less inclined to take the final step toward the production of nuclear weapons if it was reasonably certain that New Delhi would not do so.

Obviously the capacity of the United States to influence decision making on this vital question in most countries close to developing nuclear weapons is now limited, but it is by no means negligible and can be expanded. A necessary ingredient, however, is the amendment (and preferably removal) of the limitations imposed on the U.S. government by the 1978 act. A commitment to the continuance of American obligations and supervisory rights under the 1963 agreement with India on Tarapur, for instance, would partially revive Washington's capacity to influence decision making in

New Delhi on proliferation questions without enhancing India's capacity to produce nuclear weapons. This could be a politically expensive decision domestically for the Reagan administration, given the highly emotional and basically irrational response of the antinuclear lobby to this subject, but it is worthy of consideration. At least we can dismiss one of the more ludicrous arguments made by supporters of a ban on nuclear fuel shipments to India—namely, that this can be done without actually terminating the 1963 agreement and thus retaining the limitations imposed by that agreement on the use of plutonium from Tarapur by the Indian government. New Delhi has asserted that it will not accept that interpretation and will exercise its rights over the plutonium unhampered by any restrictions. If both governments accept this situation without further contentions, then the harm caused will be at least minimized. But the antinuclear lobby—with its aspirations to police the world—may well press for other ways in which to punish India for failing to abide by its instructions. Such suggestions must be clearly and emphatically rejected by the administration if its capacity to interact effectively with India on more important and more manageable issues is not to be seriously compromised.

The United States and India: Some Specific Issues

For nearly a quarter of a century, the lack of understanding between the United States and India has been a recurrent theme in the public statements and private complaints of leaders in both countries; occasionally added is a call for a sustained and widespread effort to expand and improve this relationship. One of the problems, however, has been finding international issues upon which the public positions of the two governments are close enough to provide the basis for cooperation. On most vital issues—the Arab-Israeli confrontation, South Africa versus black Africa, East-West security issues, international uses of the oceans, and the Nuclear Nonproliferation Treaty—the two powers take policy stances that are not easily reconciled. Since many of these are depicted as disagreements between industrialized and developing countries, the Soviet Union in contrast usually nominally supports underdeveloped countries with little or no cost to itself. Although more often than not Moscow's public statements are deceptive, they do give the appearance of a broader convergence of interests with developing countries than is really the case. There is little the United States can do about this, given both domestic and international pressures upon Washington on such matters.

It is probable, however, that the strains on the relationship between India and the United States in recent years are not so much the consequence of disagreement over these broader global issues as over regional developments within and adjacent to southern Asia. I will look at a number of these that have assumed and retained considerable importance in the current situation in southern Asia and upon which both the United States and India have to make policy responses.

U.S. Policy and the Indo-Soviet Relationship

One of the more persistent myths has been repeated so often in the American media, even in scholarly journals, that it is broadly accepted as a fact by the public. This myth is the supposedly broad congruence of interests between India and the Soviet Union, as perceived in New Delhi and Moscow, which in turn has transformed their relationship into an informal alliance in which India is generally responsive to Soviet leadership and guidance. The 1971 Treaty of Peace, Friendship, and Cooperation between the two powers is usually depicted as providing the legal foundation for this de facto alliance system while the regular consultation between the two states on economic, political, and security issues constitutes the institutional base. Contributing to this American perception of Indo-Soviet relations is the evident reluctance of most Indian officials, journalists, and even intellectuals to indulge in public discussions of the disagreements between India and the Soviet Union on a variety of issues—in contrast to the vigor and enthusiasm with which they expound upon, and often exaggerate, such differences with the United States. One obvious illustration of this is the way in which the Indians constantly harp upon the American naval presence in the Indian Ocean while classifying—quite inaccurately—the Soviet naval presence in these waters as a response to an American threat to Soviet security interests. They ignore the fact that the Soviet naval forces were first placed on regular assignment to the Indian Ocean in 1968, long before there were similar American forces in the region, except on what were usually assignments that required them to pass through the Indian Ocean.

Although the lack of balance and fairness in Indian official statements and media coverage of U.S. and Soviet roles on issues of importance to India is irritating and frustrating, it is not sufficient grounds for accepting the Indo-Soviet "alliance" as a fact of life and formulating U.S. policy accordingly. A number of other aspects of Indo-Soviet relations, beside their mutual disinclination to criticize each other publicly, are far more critical and deserve attention. Let me summarize these:

1. The friendly ties between India and the Soviet Union are very important to both powers; both will seek to avoid policies and actions on their part that threaten this relationship, but this posed less of a problem for Moscow and New Delhi prior to the Soviet military intervention in Af-

ghanistan in December 1979 than it does today. The strains are beginning to show on both sides even though these are kept below the surface as much as possible.

2. In defining its policies and role in south Asia since 1955, Moscow has generally played the role of a compliant—if occasionally dissatisfied—"client state," adapting its policies in the region to Indian directions in most crises. Soviet military intervention in Afghanistan marked a major break with the past in this respect potentially because it challenged the basic objective of India's regional policy—isolating southern Asia from direct military intervention by external powers, at least when this ran counter to India's self-proclaimed status as the dominant power in the region.

3. Several critical issues are currently subjects of fundamental disagreement between New Delhi and Moscow. These include: Soviet military intervention in Afghanistan and Moscow's overt efforts to incorporate it into the Soviet security and economic system; the Soviet threat to the integrity of Pakistan and Iran and, through them, to southwest Asia in general; Soviet efforts to undermine the nonalignment movement through its Cuban puppet; Soviet exploitation of Vietnam in Southeast Asia for its own narrow interests and at the expense of transforming that region from a zone of peace (through an agreement between Vietnam and the ASEAN states) into another area of external power confrontation; and Soviet insistence that India cooperate with Moscow's policy of containment of China at the expense of the normalization of Sino-Indian relations. Both governments still retain their old practice of avoiding direct public disagreements on these issues (though Indira Gandhi has come close on occasion). But Kosygin, Brezhnev, and several other Soviet political and military leaders did not descend on India in 1980 and 1981 merely to reconfirm publicly an alliance relationship but rather to discuss—in rather blunt language, according to some Indian sources—the serious areas of disagreement between the two states.

How should Washington respond to this situation? First and foremost, perhaps, by not assuming that the friendly relationship between India and the USSR is closer than it actually is. India is not a client state of the USSR; it is also not so heavily dependent upon the Soviets economically, politically, or militarily that it is in danger of becoming one. Although there are extensive ties between the two powers that are vital to India, New Delhi has other options that it can, and does, use freely at its own discretion and at times in the face of quiet objections from Moscow.

It is also possible that under some circumstances, which I will discuss in greater detail later, India can be of service to the informal negotiation process now under way between Washington and Moscow on Asian issues.

The U.S. government should have no compunctions about using India for such purposes if this serves its interests. This is one way that the United States could begin to rectify the unfortunate, self-defeating tendency of American policy in this area to be primarily reactive to policy initiatives by the Soviets and their allies or, in Southeast Asia, by China. Indeed, it is quite possible that Washington has more areas of agreement with New Delhi than with Beijing on some security and economic issues in Asia. One would never even suspect this, however, from the public position of the U.S. government, which speaks quietly on areas of disagreement with China but is much less reluctant to pronounce its displeasure with India's role and position on a variety of issues.

Dealing with Afghanistan

One of the few critical security issues on which there is public agreement between U.S. and Indian policy objectives concerns the Soviet military presence in Afghanistan and the demand for its withdrawal. But once again, an agreement on the goal has not induced cooperation between the two states on the policies and strategies to be used to persuade the Soviets to withdraw.

New Delhi's approach has been to espouse the use of diplomatic channels for the negotiation of a withdrawal in contrast to Washington's emphasis on military and economic sanctions to elicit the same objective. Although India has never had high expectations that its mediatory efforts—usually conducted through formal diplomacy—held much hope of success, it doubted from the beginning that the United States was prepared to make the necessary economic and military commitments or that, indeed, Afghanistan was the real object of U.S. policy. The Reagan administration's suspension of the grain embargo imposed on the USSR in 1980 for what appears in New Delhi to be purely (and rather minor) domestic political reasons supports this view. One instance in which New Delhi and Islamabad are in agreement is in suspecting that the United States' "punishment" of the USSR over Afghanistan is intended to be used to extract concessions from Moscow on subjects in dispute on other, more vital areas and issues as perceived by the U.S. government.

New Delhi has also generally opposed suggestions for substantial military assistance to the Afghan national liberation movements and has urged instead that the resistance forces be encouraged to seek a political accommodation with the Soviets and their puppet regime in Kabul. The Indians argue that this would remove the nominal reason for the Soviet intervention in Afghanistan. Such an accommodation would provide a face-saving device for a withdrawal of Soviet forces if this should become useful to the Soviets for reasons other than the resistance to their intervention in Afghanistan. To avoid providing the Soviets with further incentives for indirect or direct intervention in Pakistan or Iran, the U.S. government has also taken a negative attitude toward any substantial organized military assistance to the Afghan national liberation forces. But Washington also occasionally lauds the continuation of Afghan resistance to the Soviet invaders and discusses the possibility of military aid without offering any hope for a reasonably prompt resolution of the conflict that would serve Afghani, Pakistani, and Indian interests.

The general conclusion in both New Delhi and Islamabad is that the United States does not have an Afghanistan policy, but that, nevertheless, Washington takes a generally negative attitude toward the efforts by other powers to resolve the crisis on less-than-ideal terms. There is, moreover, the suspicion that Soviet intervention has served as a useful pretext to justify a substantial expansion of American military capabilities in southwest Asia and the Indian Ocean on terms that do not necessarily serve the interests of many of the area's states. What is required is greater clarity on U.S. objectives in the region as well as some indications of the concessions the United States may be willing to make to extract an agreement from Moscow to withdraw its forces from Afghanistan. Obviously Washington cannot be specific on such matters at this time, but at least a willingness to engage in bargaining would be seen as a step forward. A more positive public response to Indian offers to serve in a mediatory role would not undermine basic U.S. objectives in Asia and would be appreciated in New Delhi and even in Islamabad.

U.S. Arms Transfers and Security Relations with Pakistan

It was with a sense of satisfaction and relief that the government of India noted that the U.S.-Pakistani alliance system of the 1950s had become virtually nonfunctional following the 1965 and 1971 Indo-Pakistani wars and Pakistan's withdrawal from SEATO after the division of Pakistan into two sovereign states in 1971. Although the CENTO alliance continued to operate with some efficacy until the overthrow of the Shah of Iran in 1978, it was Iran rather than the United States that provided the primary support base for Pakistan within that alliance after 1965. This alliance constituted much less of a security problem for New Delhi than the earlier U.S.-supported system, particularly after the mid-1970s, when Iran sought to expand and improve its relations with India and encouraged Pakistan to do the same.

Events in Afghanistan and southwest Asia since December 1979, however, have led Washington to reconsider U.S. security relations with Pakistan through American involvement in a southern Asian security system centered around Pakistan. Both the Carter and Reagan administrations offered to revive an arms transfer program to Pakistan as part of the new security system. By mid-1981, Washington and Islamabad had reached an agreement on a five-year economic and military aid program ranging between $2.5 and $3 billion. It is still unclear, however, what will actually be included in the arms transfer program and also what the terms of any U.S. security commitment to Pakistan might be. When the subject of a renewed security relationship first arose in early 1980, Pakistan insisted upon security commitments from Washington that were broader than those that the United States arranged with Turkey in 1959. Presumably, what Islamabad wanted was a security commitment that was not limited to communist (that is, Soviet) aggression but also included security threats from the east (India). The Pakistani leadership appears to have had second thoughts about a security relationship with the United States that would constitute a formal alliance system, but it is assumed in Islamabad that a security commitment is at least implicit in an arms aid package such as the one offered by the Reagan administration.

As might be expected, New Delhi has watched this re-enactment of a déjà vu scenario from the 1950s with some apprehension. India's official position on arms transfers to Pakistan has been modified from the total opposition policy of the 1950s and 1960s to one that concedes that Pakistan has legitimate security problems that require military assistance from external sources. But any massive U.S. (or other) arms transfer program for Pakistan or one that involves highly advanced equipment and technology not presently available to the Indian military and that can only be used against the threat from the east (India) rather than from the west (USSR or Afghanistan) is beyond the tolerable level for New Delhi. The Indian military modernization program already well under way—a program that enhances Pakistan's sense of insecurity—would undoubtedly be expanded to at least match and probably surpass the improvement in Pakistan's military capacities under the U.S. aid program. The most likely result would be a widening of the gap between Indian and Pakistani military capabilities, under a much more stressful regional political environment than is currently the case.

It is hard to imagine a more retrogressive southern Asian environment than one in which New Delhi and Islamabad do not make sincere efforts to keep their respective military modernization programs within reasonable limits. The probable result of an arms transfer program to Pakistan of intolerable proportions to India would be an arms race in which Pakistan would have no alternative but to concentrate any military aid it received from the United States against what would become a greatly enhanced threat of Indian intervention, in Kashmir or elsewhere, rather than against the Soviet threat from Afghanistan. Indeed, in such circumstances Islamabad might well feel obliged to seek the best possible accommodation with the Soviets—at the expense of the Afghan national liberation forces, among others—in order to avoid a confrontation on two fronts. Moscow might be responsive, as its generous economic overtures to Pakistan in mid-1981 seem to indicate.

India's response to an "intolerable" U.S. arms transfer program to Pakistan would likely be the reduction or even abandonment of its present diversification policy in the procurement of more advanced military equipment and a return to a heavy dependence on the Soviet Union. This would be done less for security or economic reasons (though the latter are becoming increasingly important to New Delhi as its foreign exchange holdings continue to decline) than for political reasons. New Delhi considers it essential to maintain a good working relationship with Moscow on south Asian security issues for several reasons, including an interest in forestalling the resumption of efforts by the Soviets to assert a more balanced position between India and Pakistan in the subcontinent along the lines Moscow attempted from 1966 to 1970. One of the prices India paid for the Soviet abandonment of that policy in 1970 was the 1971 Indo-Soviet Treaty of Peace, Friendship, and Cooperation. What would Moscow seek to extract from New Delhi this time?

In any case, the basic principle for U.S. policy in south Asia should be the avoidance of any actions by Washington that would worsen Indo-Pakistani relations and thus increase the dangers of yet another war, which would probably be disastrous for Pakistan. There can be no security for Pakistan with the threats posed by a Soviet-dominated Afghanistan or many bargaining chips available to Islamabad in its negotiations with Moscow except in the context of a reasonably cooperative relationship with India. For Pakistan, security relations with the United States and the Islamic states of the Middle East would not be sufficient to enable Islamabad to avoid making major concessions to the Soviets at some point in the 1980s. Thus, the United States must exercise great care in defining the terms of a military transfer program to Pakistan if it is not to end up complicating rather than improving the difficult geostrategic situation in which Pakistan finds itself today. It would be both ironic and tragic if an American arms transfer program intended to strengthen Pakistan's capacity to resist Soviet pressure should result in a confrontation with India that left Islamabad with no viable option other than to accept an accommodation with Moscow on Soviet terms.

Moreover, a U.S. security commitment to Pakistan—if one should be demanded by Islamabad and conceded by Washington—should carefully avoid any obligations that would require the United States to support Pakistan in an Indo-Pakistani conflict in which, as in 1965, it is Islamabad that takes the initiative. It would also seem the better part of wisdom to refrain from pressing Islamabad to concede access rights to bases in Pakistan for American naval and air forces, no matter how attractive these may be to U.S. military leaders faced with the difficult task of establishing a credible American military capability in southern Asia. Pakistan's relations with both the USSR and India would be adversely affected in potentially dangerous ways, and it is doubtful that the advantages of access to bases would exceed the disadvantages of enhanced threats to Pakistan's internal and external security that would be the probable result. Moreover, while New Delhi would probably remain reluctant to change its present policy and concede similar base facilities to the Soviet naval forces in the Indian Ocean, the domestic political situation in India could well make some token concession, at least, appear necessary to the Gandhi government.

Let me conclude this discussion by emphasizing again that the primary objective of U.S. policy in south Asia should be the improvement of Indo-Pakistani relations in any way possible and the discouragement of situations that would provide the Soviet Union with opportunities to exploit the revival of Indo-Pakistani hostilities to its own advantage in relations with both Islamabad and New Delhi. Presumably, a military transfer program can be devised that would enhance Pakistan's defensive capabilities on both its eastern and western fronts without unduly alarming New Delhi. But an arms transfer program that encouraged those hard-line Pakistani military leaders to attempt to "settle" the Kashmir issue by military action would serve only Soviet interests. India and Pakistan have been involved in a difficult but persistent effort to expand and improve their relationship since the 1972 Simla Agreement, and limited but real progress was made from 1977 to 1979 while the Janata Party was in office in India. There has been some deterioration in the relationship since Indira Gandhi resumed the premiership in January 1980 but by no means back to the permanent confrontation that prevailed before 1971. Indeed, the visit of the Indian foreign minister to Islamabad in June 1981 and the friendly reception extended by President Zia and his government indicate that both sides would still prefer a cooperative relationship that included even foreign policy and security issues. Obviously, there are still wide areas of disagreement between the two nations, but it would be unwise for the United States to seek short-range and limited advantages for itself in its broader confrontations with the Soviet Union with policies that obstruct Indian and Pakistani efforts.

U.S.-Indian Economic Relations

One of the more incomprehensible aspects of American policy in Asia, including south Asia, has been the limited employment of economic factors under circumstances in which the opportunities exist and the results could be significant. Washington's response to threatening patterns of developments in Asia has usually been limited to military and security factors combined with some flashy but largely symbolic political gestures that are, by definition, of only limited value. The employment of economic incentives to improve the receptivity of American policy proposals in Asian capitals has been largely ignored, at least in any substantive terms. The U.S. economic aid program in Asia has been substantial and in some aspects, such as educational programs, useful for early stages of economic and political development. But most of the American aid has been of the short-term variety for such problems as food shortages. Such aid is of limited utility for developmental purposes and, perhaps, even counterproductive. The incredibly naive addition of the basic needs concept to the U.S. aid program—a welfare approach that is essentially antidevelopmental in effect—would have further undermined the usefulness of the aid programs if it were not for the agility with which most of the recipient governments added a basic needs supplement to their U.S.-aided development programs, raising the costs of these programs somewhat but not destroying them completely.

In any case, at this stage in most Asian countries it is not the official U.S. aid programs but the United States' role in international economic organizations and, possibly even more important, the contributions of the U.S. private sector, actual and potential, that are of primary importance. American multinational corporations have already played vital roles in the remarkable economic development of South Korea, Taiwan, and Singapore though, as often as not, in spite of rather than because of U.S. government policy. In southern Asian countries, such as India, Malaysia, Pakistan, and Indonesia, what is most required now are technological transfers rather than massive capital inputs, although capital would also be useful. American companies have so far demonstrated considerable reluctance to invest in India and Pakistan, in part because of their oppressive regulatory systems, which bewilder and discourage even the most experienced business leaders. But there are signs of liberalization on foreign investments in both states, particularly in fields that involve transfers of sophisticated technology—the oil and natural gas project in the Bay of Bengal, for example. The U.S. government can contribute to this private aid by encouraging American companies to get involved and by realistic negotiations with south Asian governments on the terms of investments. It should also avoid the illiberality that is becoming an increasing feature of U.S. trade policy with such countries as India to the advantage perhaps of some narrow economic interest groups but at the expense of most American consumers and U.S. relations with these states. Over the long run, this could well prove more important to the advancement and protection of American interests in Asia than the narrower, security-dominated mentality that has shaped U.S. policy for three decades.

Conclusion

Throughout the 1970s the U.S. government adopted a low profile in south Asia under which American economic and security aid commitments to the states of the region virtually disappeared. In part at least, this policy was based on the assumption that the expansion of Soviet influence in the subcontinent could be contained most effectively by India, the dominant power in the region and one disinclined to share its preeminent position with any external power. New Delhi was thought to be more likely to play such a role if Washington were not perceived as challenging India's regional hegemony as it had in the past. By the end of the decade, however, Washington was once again gravely concerned about the viability of Pakistan as a nation as well as New Delhi's failure to dissuade Moscow from direct military intervention in Afghanistan. The United States is seeking to devise a coherent policy that protects basic American interests in adjacent areas of southern Asia without an overcommitment, in Washington's view, of U.S. resources and obligations in the subcontinent. Let me conclude with a brief discussion of several factors that are integral to U.S. policy formulation, both within the broader Asian context and in south Asia.

It is essential that American policy should not react solely or even primarily to Soviet policies and actions as it has done in the past decade. This has proved to be self-defeating and has confused both our friends in Asia as well as the Soviet Union and its friends concerning American intentions—in particular, the limits of U.S. indulgence of Soviet expansionism. Washington must seek to create a policy environment in southern Asia in which, on occasion at least, Moscow has to react to American initiatives. The rejection of Brezhnev's zone of peace proposal for the Persian Gulf was quite proper, but it is a sad commentary on the indecisiveness and ethnocentrism prevalent in Washington that the American government has had nothing positive to offer in response.

A variety of opportunities are available in both the region of India, Pakistan, Iran, and Afghanistan and in the confrontations of ASEAN, Indochina, and China for the United States to contribute to the resolution of disputes in ways that do not constitute a sellout to the Soviet Union and its allies. The U.S. response to date, however, has been straight out of the 1950s—offers to revive military aid and security agreements combined with a proclivity for strong language and little substance in declarations of policy. Military aid is justified, indeed necessary, but the general impression in southern Asian countries appears to be that Washington is once again about to embark upon a program of security commitments in a frivolous frame of reference, without proper consideration of the long-term consequences and costs to the United States and to those states that respond favorably to American overtures and proposals.

The relationship with India has not yet deteriorated to a new low level despite America's offers of arms and technological assistance to both Pakistan and China. But the highly exaggerated rhetoric used with respect to U.S. security relations with Beijing and Islamabad is certain to revive apprehensions in New Delhi about a U.S.-China-Pakistan axis that will be seen as more threatening to India than to the Soviet Union. In current Indian strategic literature, this combination of three unfriendly powers in and around south Asia requires a Soviet-Indian axis as a counterforce, even though this would undermine New Delhi's bargaining position with Moscow at a crucial time. It is my impression that the Reagan administration is not interested in a security system involving Beijing and Islamabad that could properly be characterized as an axis and certainly not one that is directed in any way at India. But Washington has been unwilling to make this clear to everyone concerned, including India, as it strives to rebuild the image of the United States as a powerful and credible force in the international politics of Asia and the Indian Ocean.

Notes

1. Baldev Raj Nayar, "Treat India Seriously," *Foreign Policy*, no. 18 (Spring 1975): 133–54.

2. Jonathan Pollack, "The Implications of Sino-American Normalization," *International Security* 3, no. 4 (Spring 1979): 37–57.

4 | TOWARD A U.S. SECURITY POLICY IN SOUTHEAST ASIA: A MARITIME EMPHASIS

Sheldon W. Simon

U.S. security interests in Southeast Asia should be conceived as components of a global posture applied within a regional framework. Security policies toward the region, then, should further global goals, but they must be framed to take account of local political conditions. Washington should work toward resolving regional issues and problems that obstruct American strategic ends.

America's strategic concerns over the next several years as they apply to Southeast Asia center on the waters of the region—particularly the maintenance of open sea-lanes from the Persian Gulf and Indian Ocean through the China Sea. Freedom of the seas serves a number of American ends, including (1) the promotion of both U.S. trade with the Asian Pacific, which now exceeds America's European commerce, and U.S. investment in the region, which has the highest growth rate of all American capital export; (2) unimpeded waterways available to Japan, America's key Asian ally and economic partner, so it can obtain the petroleum necessary to fuel its economy; and (3) sustaining other Asian states, including the ASEAN countries (Indonesia, Singapore, Malaysia, Thailand, and the Philippines), South Korea, and Taiwan, which all trade through Asian waters to maintain their economic and political viability.

Southeast Asian regional conflicts that could impede freedom of navigation and commerce should be seen as potential obstacles to U.S. security and receive priority attention. Other conflicts, involving internal political and economic issues removed from international trade concerns, should occupy lower priority in Washington's strategic assessments. These latter disputes, while clearly important to the political futures of the countries involved, are much less susceptible to American influence. Moreover, they could lead the United States into political quicksand brought about by fruitless attempts to support one or another faction in domestic wrangles within friendly states.

The Asian Security Setting

While America's political profile in Southeast Asia remained low after 1975, that of the Soviet Union rose. By 1980, the USSR appeared to have "successfully" intervened in Angola, Ethiopia, South Yemen, Indochina, and Afghanistan, while building its Pacific fleet to a level that created concern about the ability of America's naval fleet to guarantee freedom of movement in international waters in the event of a confrontation.

The third Indochina war, beginning with Vietnam's invasion of Kampuchea (Cambodia) and followed almost immediately thereafter by China's invasion of Vietnam, brought the Sino-Soviet conflict directly into Southeast Asia and created a serious regional threat to America's maritime security goal. For the first time, as a result of its alliance with Vietnam, the Russians had military ports of call, or bases, in the South China Sea at Cam Ranh Bay, Bien Hoa, Da Nang, Haiphong, and perhaps even Kompong Som in Kampuchea.

These disturbing developments were further complicated by China's decision to advocate an alignment with the United States, Japan, and ASEAN against the USSR and Vietnam, thus attempting to associate American and ASEAN strategic interests with those of China. By declaring that its invasion into Vietnam's northern provinces served to protect Thailand against further Vietnamese movements west, China has created a sense of dependency in Bangkok, which serves only to solidify the polarization of regional politics and makes more intractable the Soviet-Vietnamese connection.

Washington has maneuvered itself into an unfortunate position. By aligning with China, as Washington increasingly demonstrated with the Brzezinski and Harold Brown visits to Beijing in 1978 and 1979, its international actions and official declarations became increasingly associated with China's antihegemony posture. Consequently, America's relations with the USSR have worsened and probably have accounted for Soviet efforts to expand Soviet influence in Asia.

Managing relations with China and the Soviet Union has presented a challenge for some years. But, the trend has been favorable for the United States. The disintegration of the Sino-Soviet alliance and rapprochement with China permitted the United States to change its strategy for fighting more than one war at a time. Thus, since extricating itself from Indochina, Washington has not faced the prospect of a land war in Asia. Air and naval contingents are the forces on which America relies to reassure friendly states of assistance against threats of external aggression. More important than the military utility of these forces, however, is their political meaning. They symbolize a continued American commitment to Asia's integrity and hence permit its members to remain independent of pressures from Moscow and Beijing to choose sides. If the United States appears to line up with China, as it has since Vietnam's incursion into Kampuchea, smaller states in the region may believe that their maneuverability is constrained—hence the general lack of enthusiasm among the ASEAN states for strong ties among China, the United States, and Japan.

Southeast Asia's Importance

While abjuring direct military intervention in Third World confrontations, the Carter administration, nevertheless, assisted friendly regional powers in Southeast Asia through modest military and economic aid programs. ASEAN members were particularly singled out as an incipient security group whose policies encouraged international trade and investment. Support for strong noncommunist governments fit America's future vision of Asia. In effect, a successful ASEAN was precisely the kind of regional group the United States had hoped to foster in its ill-fated defense of South Vietnam. Indochina had since come within Vietnamese sphere of control (some would say—incorrectly—Russian); but the ASEAN states remained independent, cooperative, and staunchly opposed to all brands of communism, be they Russian, Chinese, or Vietnamese.

Not surprisingly, Washington has centered its Southeast Asian security hopes on ASEAN. Insofar as America proclaims a security policy in this region, its goal is to help maintain ASEAN's independence and promote its members' development. This vision is complicated, however, because a hotly contested war continues—along Thailand's eastern border. Should Thailand become embroiled in these Indochinese conflicts, ASEAN and U.S. security interests would be affected. The key question is whether local hostilities can be contained (and hence U.S. security interests reduced) when China and the USSR are backing the contenders. Since military tension also persists along the China-Vietnam frontier and along the lengthy Sino-Soviet border, Southeast Asian hostilities are linked to the Sino-Soviet conflict and the Sino-Soviet-American triangle.

As long as local war persists on the Southeast Asian mainland, the region's attention and resources are diverted from developing a maritime capacity to help maintain the unimpeded flow of international commerce through Southeast Asian waterways. Moreover, continuation of the ASEAN-Vietnam confrontation provides the opportunity for both China and the Soviet Union to use each contender against the other. This situation is particularly beneficial for the Soviets, since it gives them leverage to expand their use of Vietnamese bases in exchange for continued military aid. If the ASEAN-Vietnam dispute remains at a relatively low military level, then it is unlikely that the USSR will pressure Hanoi to compromise. Indeed, the conflict's continuation is probably preferred in Moscow as long as no direct Soviet military involvement is contemplated.

China, on the other hand, is most dissatisfied with the current alliance structure in Southeast Asia and least able to affect its outcome. Its greatest desire is to see the Soviet-Vietnamese relationship disrupted and Indochina restored to the former status of three small, separate states. Beijing urges the creation of a large anti-Soviet front of Asian noncommunist states united with Washington. In the face of such overwhelming opposition, Hanoi presumably would sever its Soviet connection to avoid diplomatic isolation—though the Chinese acknowledge this outcome may take several years to achieve. To encourage the formation of a broadly based anti-Soviet conglomeration, China has virtually abdicated the leadership of worldwide radical, agrarian revolution, turned a blind eye to issues of social injustice in the Third World, and has been ready to associate with any government willing to classify the USSR as its primary enemy. (Even John Foster Dulles would probably have accepted a China with this orientation.)

The Soviets, however, were appalled at what they perceived to be the formation of a Sino-Japanese-U.S. entente attendant upon the Sino-Japanese Friendship Treaty of 1978. Given a generally paranoid view of world politics, Soviet leaders interpreted the antihegemony rhetoric emanating from Washington, Tokyo, and Beijing as a coordinated effort designed to exclude the USSR from any role in Asian affairs—an unrealistic prospect, given Russia's growing Pacific fleet. Moscow's subsequent friendship treaty with Vietnam was a kind of political insurance against the tripartite union the Soviets believed had formed against them. Seen in this light, the treaty with Vietnam and renewed publicity for a proposed Asian collective security system were Russia's way of buying back into regional affairs. After all, the essence of the Asian collective security concept was that all Asian states must be involved in regional security arrangements.

China's limited incursion into Vietnam, following the latter's early-1979 occupation of Kampuchea, proved serendipitous for the Russians because it gave them the opportunity to expand their use of Vietnamese ports and airfields at a time when the Soviet Pacific fleet was searching for new locations on the South China Sea.

Hanoi, by contrast, resisted Soviet requests for affiliation with its Eastern European allies and base rights for three years, succumbing only when the Soviets agreed to support Vietnam's plan to invade Kampuchea. The cost of this bargain for the Russians has been considerable. It seriously set back relations with China when the Russians were hoping to improve them; it exacerbated relations with the United States, undermining ratification of the Strategic Arms Limitation Treaty, and—worst of all—provided an incentive for China, the United States, and ASEAN to move together against the Soviet regional buildup. No longer do the Russians badger the ASEAN states to close American bases in the Philippines when Russian ships and aircraft regularly ply the waters of Cam Ranh Bay and use American-built air facilities at Da Nang.

America's strategic interest is clearly not served by the Soviet-Vietnam alliance. But Washington's ability to weaken that relationship appears extremely limited. By associating with China's antihegemony policy and assisting in its overall modernization, Washington serves to drive Hanoi closer to Moscow. Increased military aid to the ASEAN states and America's enhanced Seventh Fleet and Thirteenth Air Force capabilities in the region will similarly strengthen Russian-Vietnamese ties.

This hardening of political relationships was not inevitable. Until 1978, ASEAN states encouraged Washington to establish relations with Vietnam to provide an alternative to the latter's dependence on the USSR. But Vietnam's crisis with Kampuchea and its reliance on Soviet military support to settle the conflict, as well as the priority given to establishing relations with China, led to a shift in the Carter administration's policy toward China and accelerated Southeast Asia's realignment. Thus, Vietnam's invasion of Cambodia had the surprising effect of seemingly reviving the moribund Manila Treaty, in whose name Washington sped the delivery of military aid to Thailand.

American policy changes toward Asia since 1975 appear reactive and inconsistent and lack a strategic framework.[1] Those who preferred a low profile and reduced American commitments argued that rapprochement with China left only the USSR as a regional adversary, and Moscow's political position in Asia is weak. With only one reluctant ally (Vietnam) characterized by a strong commitment to independence, the Soviets will not be able to manipulate the relationship to their advantage. Thus, the United States need not waste its own resources by attempting to counter an already overextended USSR. Instead, these minimalists argue, Washington should phase out its military installations from the Philippines, moving them to the United States' mid-Pacific territories. The minimalists ignore, however, that America is a Pacific power with the bulk of its trade and rapidly growing investment carried out in that region. Moreover, because Japan depends on Southeast Asian shipping lanes for almost all of its petroleum, the Seventh Fleet serves to protect vital commercial waterways.

An opposing school of thought to that of the minimalists is represented by those who advocate a united front strategy. This concept is based on the belief that the Soviets are a genuine threat to Asia but that the United States should no longer be required to meet that threat alone. Instead, Washington should create the broadest possible united front against the Soviet Union, including Japan, China, and the ASEAN states. (This, in effect, has been Chinese strategy since 1978.) The problem with this approach is that it would further exacerbate tensions with the USSR and tend to force Soviet-American relations back into the 1950s cold war mold. Moreover, American support for China's united front could have the unintended effect (from Washington's perspective) of abetting the creation of Chinese hegemony in the region which, in turn, could lead to fissures within ASEAN. Malaysia and Indonesia are at least as suspicious of China as they are of Vietnam. Furthermore, neither of these approaches would facilitate the creation of an environment that would lead either to a reduction of Soviet base facilities in Vietnam or a consensus within the region about the necessity of maintaining open sea and air lanes.

Prior to 1978 and the development of open tensions between ASEAN-China and Vietnam-USSR, the Carter administration seemed to be moving toward a minimalist pattern. This was particularly evident in the Seventh Fleet's so-called swing strategy by which U.S. naval units would be transferred to Europe in the event of an emergency. The swing policy raised questions about the seriousness of the United States' commitment to Asia, especially in light of the growth of the Soviets' Pacific fleet. Nineteen seventy-eight proved to be something of a watershed year. Washington made a number of gestures to show it would not withdraw from Asia. Vice-President Walter Mondale visited the Philippines, Thailand, and Indonesia. New aid agreements were signed in Bangkok and Jakarta, and serious negotiations led subsequently to a renewal of the agreement regarding U.S. bases in the Philippines. In the spring of 1980, the Department of Defense dropped the swing strategy, stating that the growing Soviet naval threat to Pacific sea-lanes and the tensions in the Persian Gulf attendant upon the Soviet invasion of Afghanistan, as well as the Soviet use of Vietnamese bases, make it imperative that the Seventh Fleet remain at full strength. In effect, the United States had acknowledged that the Middle East and Asia had acquired an importance to the United States equal to that of Europe.

Threats to U.S. Security Interests in Southeast Asia

Three threatening environments in Southeast Asia could undermine regional stability and adversely effect American relations with regional members. Each should be assessed according to its effect on a U.S. maritime emphasis proposed in this chapter. In descending order of imminence, they include:

1. The prospect of Vietnamese military operations against the Khmer opposition spilling over into Thailand in the course of hot pursuit or as a premeditated step to force Khmer resistance enclaves further into Thailand and away from the Cambodian border. (The June 1980 incursion had this latter end in mind.)
2. Indigenous insurgencies opposed to incumbent authoritarian regimes in the Philippines, Thailand, or Indonesia increasing during the 1980s as development strategies disproportionately benefit urban elites affiliated with transnational enterprises at the expense of the masses, who frequently live at rural subsistence levels.
3. The possibility over time of the Soviet Pacific fleet attempting to interdict Southeast Asian straits or harass Japanese shipping from bases in Vietnam and Kampuchea. Russian ships, particularly if large carriers with marine contingents are among them, could also deter noncommunist (that is, ASEAN and American) intervention to protect friendly governments against Soviet-Vietnamese-backed insurgencies.

ASEAN's primary concern is the Vietnamese occupation of Kampuchea and the political chain reaction that followed. The Soviet Union now has a close ally in the region for the first time. Its ships and planes regularly use Vietnam's ports and airfields to secure the USSR's own trade and fishing activities in the area, as well as to monitor the military activities and defense preparations of littoral states. Given the general consensus that U.S. forces will not intervene in mainland Southeast Asia again, Thailand has reluctantly come to expect another Chinese attack upon Vietnam. This is a particularly uncomfortable situation for Malaysia and Indonesia, which see China's ambitions to be as much a cause of regional instability as Vietnam's ambitions. An early casualty of these developments has been ASEAN's hopes for the creation of a zone of peace, freedom, and neutrality for Southeast Asia by which the noncommunist states of the region hoped to insulate regional affairs from the machinations of military activities by larger powers. With Soviet forces operating out of Da Nang, Bien Hoa and Cam Ranh Bay, ASEAN states have not only called on the United States to maintain its Seventh Fleet in the region but also may contemplate the possibility of an enhanced Japanese naval escort force, which could operate in conjunction with the Seventh Fleet up to the Strait of Malacca. Japanese Self-Defense Force Director-General Jōji Omura has acknowledged that Japan's sea-lanes are vulnerable to the strengthened Soviet naval presence, which ranges from the western Pacific through the Indian Ocean.[3] From Cam Ranh Bay, Soviet bombers are within two hours of the Strait of Malacca and can easily monitor military movements in Subic Bay and around the south China coast. Moreover, Soviet military ships have used Vietnamese harbors since 1980 on what appear to be Russian regional missions, as distinct from providing supplies to Vietnam.

As the USSR strengthens its presence in Vietnam, U.S. policymakers concerned with meeting and deterring the Soviet challenge have tended to respond by re-enforcing links with China and providing more military aid to the ASEAN states. These moves have given Hanoi an incentive to strengthen Soviet ties and serve to sustain the polarization of regional politics. They also portend a growing Soviet use of Vietnamese bases in exchange for the continued underwriting of Vietnam's military establishment.

The entente of China, the United States, and ASEAN against Vietnam's occupation of Kampuchea is insufficient to force a Vietnamese withdrawal, and worse, provocative enough to ensure that Vietnam remains closely tied to the USSR. At best, the entente might cause the Vietnamese to lengthen their timetable for wiping out resistance forces until ASEAN and the United States have lost interest and scale down their support for the resistance. However, if anti-Vietnamese efforts appear to be adding to Khmer resistance strength or seem to be expanding Thai sanctuaries for Laotian and Cambodian groups, the Vietnamese could be tempted to move preemptively across the Thai border. It is unlikely, however, that Hanoi has the capacity for a sustained assault on Thailand as long as China threatens Vietnam's northern border. Estimates in 1981 placed 60 percent of the Vietnamese People's Army between Hanoi and the Chinese frontier.[4]

External threats to Southeast Asia, then, center on the mainland. Vietnam's main fear is that China wishes to restore its position in Kampuchea through the Khmer Rouge or a new coalition, which could be unfriendly to Hanoi. On the other hand, China's opposition to Vietnamese control of Indochina centers on the military relationship between Hanoi and Moscow. ASEAN is involved because of Vietnam's incipient threat to Thailand either through direct military incursion or long-range assistance to ethnic groups in Thailand's northeastern region. From an American strategic perspective, while the conflict on mainland Southeast Asia persists, little will be done to develop a cooperative maritime capacity in the region, and the

Soviets will be guaranteed the use of Indochinese base facilities. It is clearly in America's interest to encourage regional acceptance of Vietnam's dominant position in Indochina if, in exchange, Hanoi will withdraw its military forces from the Thai border and gradually remove most of its troops from Kampuchea. Additionally, Washington and the ASEAN states should press Vietnam to impose limits on the Soviet use of its ports and airfields, confining that use to normal international commerce and military port calls, while ceasing to provide bases from which Soviet forces conduct regular missions into the South China Sea and Indian Ocean. Even if this maximum objective cannot be attained, a resolution of the ASEAN-Vietnam confrontation would help to reduce tensions within ASEAN itself over whether China or Vietnam presents the greatest threat to the region.

ASEAN Ambivalence

A major obstacle to any settlement of the mainland conflict is, of course, China's orientation toward ASEAN and Vietnam. Although ASEAN has lined up behind Thailand against Vietnam's occupation of Cambodia, it would be a gross distortion to conclude that ASEAN is in China's camp. After invasions of Kampuchea and then Vietnam, ASEAN called for withdrawal of foreign forces from both countries. ASEAN has not encouraged increased Chinese involvement in Southeast Asia. Indeed, Beijing remains volatile and unpredictable from ASEAN's perspective. At a minimum, China is seen as a rival for scarce economic aid, trade, and investment as it proceeds to modernize. Moreover, prior to the deterioration of Sino-Vietnamese relations in 1978, ASEAN states had encouraged Washington to establish relations with Hanoi in hopes of diluting Russian influence in the region and creating a more balanced presence of outside political interests on the mainland. Thailand, with ASEAN's assistance, must find a way of disengaging from China's self-proclaimed security embrace without damaging its general political relationship with Beijing.

From the American perspective, ASEAN has become an informal ally (though not an alliance partner). The United States is not obliged to assist in Thailand's defense under the Manila Treaty. But that treaty, which enables the United States to continue to maintain its bases in the Philippines, gives America some military leverage in Southeast Asia to counter any challenges from the USSR or Vietnam. Washington no longer has a regional security organization, but it retains bilateral commitments and has followed a policy since the late 1970s of backing ASEAN initiatives.

Support for ASEAN governments has created another dilemma for U.S. policymakers. Because U.S. alliance diplomacy is severely constrained in Southeast Asia, Washington's participation consists of backing friendly states. But when Washington becomes involved in supporting ASEAN incumbents, it is then identified with authoritarian regimes that, for the most part, are concerned less with social justice than with the aggregate development of their economies. Although ASEAN has been notably successful in the past decade in increasing aggregate growth rates, disparities between the poor and rich in these societies have been exacerbated. Ruling elites are narrowly based in gentry and industrial-technocratic classes and backed by the military. These kinds of political systems stress stability rather than participation. Insurgent threats resulting from irredentism, regional autonomy demands, and more organized resistance by those who see themselves as deprived under these arrangements are met through a variety of authoritarian methods of suppression. Frequently, appeals for reform are ignored or branded as communist-inspired. Most of the ASEAN societies, then, could be political time bombs. If revolution occurs in, say, the Philippines or Thailand, Washington's position in the region could change overnight because of its close ties to the ancien régime.

Nevertheless, the United States has little choice but to deal with friendly governments as they exist despite the inevitability of succession crises in authoritarian political systems, the shallowness of their political institutions, and alternating bouts between authoritarian and revolutionary violence. On the positive side, all ASEAN governments are pursuing nationalist development strategies. New elites in science, management, and technology are emerging to apply the extraordinary advances of recent decades in the fields of industry, agriculture, and population control. ASEAN's potential for growth is particularly heartening. In aggregate economic terms, it has been one of the most successful regions of the world for the past ten years. If Indonesia, Malaysia, Thailand, and the Philippines succeed in diversifying and decentralizing their light industrial bases while developing agricultural credit systems that permit farmers to stay on their land, the social revolutionary pressures predicted in the previous paragraph could be ameliorated.

Despite these long-range concerns, American relations with ASEAN in the early 1980s are close and cordial. The association has provided its five members with the diplomatic strength required to maintain "independent" foreign policies while drawing close to Japan and the United States as donor countries. Frequent ASEAN consultations on political and economic issues have forged a diplomatic united front. Moreover, these consultations mean that each member develops a stake in the other's success and tries to accommodate the others' needs. ASEAN external relations, then, are cautious and consensual. The association tends to defer to the member country whose interests seem to be most involved, as, for example, Thailand, with respect to the Vietnamese occupation of Kampuchea. But because the military capabilities of the five countries are insufficient to meet external threats, reliance on American deterrence in the forms of U.S. Pacific air and naval power constitute the unstated basic premise of ASEAN security.

Nevertheless, growing nationalism among ASEAN members and skepticism over the credibility of America's willingness to defend them against potential aggressors have begun to elicit the gradual buildup of their own external defense capabilities. Given the strategic argument of this chapter, which centers on shared abilities to monitor and maintain oceanic freedom, the United States should welcome and assist these efforts.

Toward this end, ASEAN military expenditures have increased enormously in recent years.[5] In 1980, they totaled $5.5 billion, a 45 percent increase over 1979 and nearly double the amount spent in 1975. Over the past five years, U.S. military aid to ASEAN increased 250 percent compared with the first half of the 1970s, from $327 million to $820 million. Commercial arms sales from the United States to ASEAN armed forces between 1977 and 1980 also skyrocketed to $2.48 billion from $1.12 billion during 1970 to 1977. Although much of this aid has been diverted to counterinsurgency, recent spending has been allocated for such new strategic items as Malaysian and Indonesian air bases and modern naval weapons systems whose ultimate use would be to project military power beyond national boundaries to protect vital sea routes and monitor regional military movements.

Such capability is still distant. In the early 1980s, ASEAN's combined military forces totaled less than 700 thousand while Vietnam alone had a military establishment of more than one million battle-hardened troops. ASEAN militaries, by contrast, have never fought a conventional war. The two largest ASEAN armies—those of Indonesia and Thailand—have about one-third of their personnel involved in civil and administrative duties. There is little arms standardization, no common training or command systems, and, of course, no common language. Some bilateral joint naval and air exercises occur, but they have never included full-scale maneuvers or war games that would, for example, include multinational air-ground combat coordination.

Were Thailand to be subjected to a full-scale Vietnamese attack in the near future, it is unlikely that ASEAN could do much militarily to assist. Malaysian and Philippine capabilities are largely limited to handling domestic insurgencies, while Indonesia has little to spare in the way of ammunition and equipment and would be hard pressed to provide even a combat-ready battalion. The one area in which some joint progress has been made is the air force. All ASEAN air forces will be using F-5E jets, which have interception and ground attack capabilities, within the next few years. Joint air exercises have led to some standardization in weaponry and operational doctrine.

In general, the ASEAN states prefer to see both Chinese and Vietnamese influence reduced in Southeast Asia. ASEAN's argument to Vietnam is that by withdrawing its forces from Kampuchea and accepting a neutral coalition government, Chinese influence would atrophy. Subsequently, Vietnam could regain its independent foreign policy, including American reconstruction aid. But, under Gen. Prem Tinsulanond, the prime minister, Thailand seems to have lost sight of this strategy and is opposing Vietnam's occupation of Kampuchea as an end in itself. This plays into Hanoi's hands, for it charges that Thailand is a principal in the conflict since it supplies and provides sanctuary for the Khmer resistance.

A major task for American diplomacy in Southeast Asia, then, is to encourage resolution of the Indochina-ASEAN confrontation. Washington should hold intensive private discussions initially with Thailand, and subsequently other ASEAN states, stressing the fruitlessness of a continued standoff with Vietnam and urging acceptance of Hanoi's domination of Indochina, which could reduce China's pressure on ASEAN for alignment as well as provide an opportunity for Vietnam to become less dependent on the USSR. By terminating assistance to the Khmer Rouge, Bangkok would demonstrate its goodwill to Vietnam. Hanoi has indicated that such a policy from Thailand would lead to the withdrawal of its forces from the Thai border. Reduction of the direct Vietnamese threat to Thailand, in turn, would permit the other ASEAN states to enter into negotiations with Hanoi, which might restore normal relations among them and lead to an understanding about the reduction of the Soviet presence in Indochina. This reduction could be negotiated in exchange for American and Japanese reconstruction assistance.

The major obstacle to the realization of this scenario is, of course, China. Beijing, in effect, would be the big loser if these developments were to unfold. Thus, China, too, would have to be persuaded that accommodating Vietnam would be a more effective way of ultimately limiting the Vietnam-Soviet relationship than continuing to bleed Hanoi by its direct military action or any support for the Khmer Rouge. It is unlikely, however, that China will accept this logic because its dispute with Vietnam is not confined to the latter's Russian tie but is also the product of a strong historical pattern. Keeping a smaller, neighboring state in a subordinate position is central to China's regional view. From China's perspective, Vietnam is a recalcitrant tributary and must be taught a lesson. But there is no reason for ASEAN or the United States to become involved in its implementation.

Conclusions: Toward a Maritime Security Pattern

Between 1945 and 1975, the baseline for U.S. military personnel in Asia remained stable at about 180 thousand. By the end of the 1970s, withdrawals from Thailand, Korea, Taiwan, and some reduction in Seventh Fleet personnel had lowered that figure to less than 130 thousand, the lowest level since 1939. Nevertheless, the United States has continually given its backing for Japanese and Korean security, bilateral security ties to the Philippines and Thailand, the ANZUS treaty, and the maintenance of freedom of the seas in the Indian Ocean, South China Sea, and Sea of Japan.

The 1980s have begun with a clear Soviet commitment to deploy its Pacific Fleet in the Asian seas, which had previously been an American monopoly. Long-term Sino-Vietnamese tensions, which exacerbate pressures on the ASEAN states to choose sides between China and the USSR, provide a strong justification for a U.S. strategy that defends the Asian Pacific basin. With U.S. bases in Japan, Korea, and the Philippines, a quick-reaction capability serves to deter Soviet intervention and hence relieves the weight on ASEAN to line up either behind or against one of the Sino-Soviet antagonists. In effect, the maintenance of U.S. forces in the Pacific Ocean near Asia permits the ASEAN states to sustain independent foreign policies. Any pulling back of U.S. naval and air forces from the Philippines to the mid-Pacific in the Asian strategic environment of the 1980s would degrade Washington's ability to project and sustain naval and air power into the South China Sea and Indian Ocean. It would, therefore, reduce its utility to ASEAN and Japan. And U.S. air power in the Philippines not only serves the southern Asian perimeter but also is a logistical base for Korea, Japan, and Diego Garcia. In this light, it is noteworthy that members of the organized democratic opposition to Philippine President Ferdinand Marcos have stated that they, too, would honor the current U.S.-Philippine bases agreement if the opposition succeeds in removing Marcos from office.[6]

The probable American contribution to Southeast Asian security for the 1980s will be neither as ubiquitous as in the 1960s and early 1970s nor as minimal as most skeptics contend. Washington will retain significant and sophisticated air and naval forces in the region despite growing financial costs, to balance the Soviet buildup. Unlike the 1960s, however, the United States will not attempt to assist incumbent governments in coping with their internal security problems or localized frontier defense concerns—with the exception of the sale of military equipment and provision of training. Rather, America's direct security role will be confined to protecting regional allies in the unlikely event of external conventional attack and maintaining the freedom of sea and air lanes.

But the United States should no longer be required to engage in regional defense by itself. A growing Japanese navy can assist in monitoring the waters around Japan's home islands. Australia has inaugurated Indian Ocean patrols, and Malaysia and Indonesia have begun to acquire the air and naval units needed to monitor the seas around their shores as well.

If ASEAN rejects the prospect of Japan deploying its ships to escort tankers to the Straits of Malacca, Lombok, and Sunda, then at least Malaysia and Indonesia should develop their own abilities to keep these waters open to international commerce in cooperation with the U.S. Seventh Fleet. The Philippines, too, may well have the incentive to engage in naval surveillance as the decade proceeds; it is concerned with staking its claim to part of the Spratly islands in contention with Vietnam. Toward this end the Philippine air force has recently purchased surveillance aircraft.

All of these capacities serve an American maritime security interest and should be supported by Washington through the provision of military credits and sales on easy terms. The 1980s portend, then, not a U.S. military withdrawal from Southeast Asia but a strategy emphasizing air and naval deployments in cooperation with friendly states to maintain the freedom of commercial routes and to deter Soviet or Vietnamese expansionary designs.

Notes

1. Much of the following discussion is drawn from Robert Scalapino, "Approaches to Peace and Security in Asia: The Uncertainty Surrounding American Strategic Principles," in Sudershan Chawla and D. R. Sardesai, eds., *Changing Patterns of Security and Stability in Asia* (New York: Praeger, 1980). Pages 1–5 are especially useful.

2. Possibilities of threats are discussed at some length in Sheldon W. Simon's *The ASEAN States and Regional Security* (Stanford: Hoover Institution Press, 1982).

3. *Kyodo,* October 21, 1980, in Foreign Broadcast Information Service (FBIS), *Daily Report Asia/Pacific,* October 21, 1980, p. C1.

4. Russell Briggs, "China's Bulwark Against Asia's New Imperialists," *Christian Science Monitor,* February 3, 1981.

5. The following data may be found in Ho Kwon-Ping and Cheah Cheng-Hye, "Five Fingers on the Trigger," *Far Eastern Economic Review,* October 24, 1980, pp. 32–37. All dollar figures are quoted in current terms and, therefore, do not account for inflation.

6. *Agence France Press* (Hong Kong) January 22, 1981, in FBIS, *Daily Report Asia/Pacific,* January 22, 1981, p. 1.

5 | JAPAN AND NORTHEAST ASIA

Donald C. Hellmann

Two issues will be central to U.S. foreign policy toward Asia and the Pacific in the 1980s and beyond: (1) the priority given to Asia in a long-term global strategic policy and (2) the development of an appropriate new posture in regard to Japan, a country on the threshold of a new, major role in the region and the world. The issues are integrally linked, but require separate treatment to be seen in proper perspective. Policymakers and specialists alike regularly acknowledge the critical importance of Asia in our approach to the world, but despite three major wars in the past four decades and trade relations that have long surpassed Europe in size, American policy toward this region does not receive the attention or priority appropriate to Asia's current status and future potential. The United States' policy toward Asia tends to proceed in an ad hoc and incremental fashion, essentially in passive response to international events. Actual policy choices have been cast in terms of a strategic vision of global containment held over from the 1950s and 1960s when the situation in Asia and the capacity of the United States to deal with it were significantly different. During the 1970s, policy proceeded in the shadow of the debacle in Vietnam or in accordance with a rather romanticized approach to normalizing relations with China. There have been some disastrous failures and some truly notable diplomatic triumphs, but, in aggregate, progress has been sporadic and reactive. "Wanted: An Asian Policy" is as appropriate a plea today as it was 30 years ago, but this cannot continue in the future.

In particular, four international realities make essential the development of a coherent Asian policy with a central place in America's overall approach to the world: (1) the vastly increased capacities of all countries in the region (for example, Taiwan, South Korea, and Indonesia as well as China and Japan) to act independently in strategic and economic affairs; (2) the confluence of economics and political-strategic affairs as a result of the astonishing prosperity that has affected virtually all noncommunist nations in this area; (3) a significantly enhanced Soviet military presence in the region and its impact on Sino-American relations; and (4) basic uncertainties about the future role of Japan, now the world's second largest industrial power, in the region and the world.

Asia should hold a more prominent position in American global policy, and Japan should be the foundation of our policy toward Asia. Partly because of the remarkable success of the Japanese-American alliance and the turmoil that has been associated with virtually all other aspects of our involvement in Asia and partly because of the persistent sirenlike attraction of China, Japanese policy has not been given the appropriate attention or priority it deserves. In large part because the United States has insulated the Japanese from the pressures of international politics, Japan has been allowed to sit on the sidelines of global and regional strategic-military affairs without any real foreign policy beyond dependence on the American alliance. At the same time, American credibility as an economic as well as a military superpower steadily eroded in the 1970s.

The Japanese enter the 1980s with enormously expanded wealth, but without a clear, realistic set of foreign policy goals and with considerable domestic political fluidity. The United States can constructively influence a new direction in bilateral relations with the only democratic industrialized power in the region, but the United States must have a more coherent policy toward Asia and the world if it is to be viable in the long run. What is proposed here may be called an "Asia first, Japan first policy."

American Diplomatic Priorities: Asia First?

Despite the fact that east Asia has been at the center of American diplomatic concerns for most of recent history, the region still does not receive the considered attention and continuing priority that has been accorded to Western Europe and the Middle East—far less than that lavished on global containment of the Soviet Union. Rather, American involvement in Asia has been sporadic and volatile, touched by an emotionalism born of the anguish of war and a romantic attachment to complex, rapidly changing societies neither Western nor fully understood. Viewed historically, Asia would seem to deserve top priority in long-term American strategic goals. Since 1940, the United States has fought three major wars in this region, has lavished more aid on Asian countries than on those in any other area of the world, and, for some years now, has done more trade with east Asian nations than with the European Economic Community. To understand why in the face of this cumulative experience the United States still lacks a sophisticated and unequivocal commitment to the region, it is necessary to look first at the nature of American domestic politics.

East Asia has been the scene of the greatest frustrations and failures in American diplomacy since World War II: the loss of China to the Communists in the late 1940s, the costly and disappointing stalemate in the limited Korean War, and the decade-long debacle in Vietnam. All of these events profoundly affected domestic politics in the United States, especially the Vietnam War. The traumatic impact of this war shattered the postwar foreign policy consensus, deeply touched the careers and personal lives of a generation of Americans, and still fundamentally shapes the parameters for a credible and effective strategic posture in Asia. One of the legacies of these disappointing American excursions into the politics of east Asia is an extreme reluctance to risk failure again by becoming centrally involved in the turbulent international affairs of this region. This reflex isolationism has cast a pall over relations with such countries as Japan and South Korea with which the United States is deeply and inextricably bound. Another legacy of the United States' sporadic deep involvement in Asia has been to exacerbate the emotionalism that has long characterized our approach to this part of the world, especially China.

An element of morality and romanticism has colored our relations with China and other Asian nations in ways that continue to inhibit the formulation of an informed and realistic policy. China for centuries has been an object of bewilderment, fascination, and concern to the Western world. The cultural and ideological distance that separates Americans from the traditional Chinese society, as well as revolutionary communism, plus the perception that major historical forces are at work for all to see on one-fourth of humanity, underlies the volatility and extremism, the attraction and revulsion that has characterized our policies toward China and Taiwan for the past 35 years. Finally, America's foreign policy toward China has always contained an element of self-righteous dispensing of aid and advice, which invariably produced bitterness on the American side because the Chinese never responded or behaved according to American expectations. This moral overtone in American diplomatic relations toward China could never produce a realistic long-term policy.

In addition to the bitterness, guilt, and anguish regarding Vietnam and the romantic attachment to China, a moralism is also associated with our policies toward Japan and Korea. Because of the extraordinary impact of the American occupation and the close ties that have grown during the following decades in the remarkably successful Japanese-American alliance, a special and emotional relationship (in this case reciprocal) has developed with Japan. This relationship has a paternalistic cast, and like the father who rejoices in the self-image seen in a successful son, the United States, until the past decade, has tended to view the alliance as resting on principles that transcended narrow calculations of self-interest. Accordingly, the increased international economic success of Japan during the 1970s, often at American expense, provoked extreme reactions of contrasting hues from various sectors of American society. The bitter attacks on unfair trade practices from business as well as labor, the so-called Nixon shocks of 1971 (when Nixon opened ties with China and allowed the U.S. dollar to float relative to foreign currencies), and the more strident demands to end the free ride on defense represent the critical responses. At the other extreme is the Japanophile viewpoint represented most graphically in a 1979 book by the director of the Harvard East Asian Research Center, *Japan as Number One: Lessons for America*.[1] This argues that the current ills of the American economy, society, and polity can be solved by copying the Japanese model—that is, reversing the occupation of 35 years ago. Applied to any other bilateral relationship, all of these responses, the negative and the positive, would seem extreme if not bizarre; they suggest the need for special concern for putting Japanese-American relations on an appropriate new level.

The United States' relations with the Republic of Korea have also been predicated on a moral posture in which U.S. aid was given only on the condition that the South Koreans behave in a particular fashion. By expecting that South Korea would treat its dissidents as the U.S. government treats its critics at home, America's leaders imposed moral precepts on its foreign policy toward allies. This imposition only complicated efforts to conceive of an innovative and realistic policy toward a strategic peninsula in Asia beset by the extreme tensions between North and South Korea. Because of the war fought on behalf of South Korea, because of a remarkable success economically and as a military ally, because of deep personal ties between the Korean and American elites, and because of practices (violations of human rights, for example) at odds with American ideals, Korean policy has regularly provoked strong and extreme responses within American politics. An appreciation of this unique emotional dimension with several critical countries in the region is fundamental to the formulation of future U.S. policies toward east Asia.

Another factor in American domestic politics central to forming a new Asian policy for the 1980s and beyond is the structure of the foreign policy elite. Almost without exception, those advisers closest to the center of power in Washington have been Eurocentric in perspective or have acquired knowledge of Asia as a result of short intensive study under the pressure of crises. Without substantial background on which to make considered judgment among the critical advisers and the small group of specialists who have access to policymaking, it is understandable how policy has proceeded issue by issue toward short-term goals led by events, rather than leading them and without any concerted and serious effort to relate Asian policy to our global strategy. Moreover, in the absence of strong policy leadership, the direction of American moves was particularly shaped during the 1970s by the tangle of political forces in Washington: the mood of Congress (influenced by the War Powers Act and disclosures of Korean nationals' bribing congressmen), the pressure of interest groups lobbying for protection against Japan and other newly industrialized countries, and presidential grandstanding (through recognition of China) for domestic political purposes. Consequently, to a substantial degree the composition of the foreign policy elite has further domesticated foreign policy toward Asia by making it unusually susceptible to internal American politics.

In addition to the moralism that colors the American approach to east Asia and the predisposition of the foreign policy elites, the development of a coherent long-term Asia policy has been inhibited by the institutional arrangements for foreign policymaking. In large part this is the result of arrangements that bedevil all aspects of strategic planning: (1) the roles of the main departments and advisory bodies to the president—the Departments of State, Defense, and the Treasury and the National Security Council, for example—have varied from one administration to another, making jurisdiction over policy as well as policy itself a matter of continuing dispute; (2) the enormous pressure of the day-to-day responsibilities on the individuals who conduct our foreign policy; this pressure severely inhibits consideration of the long-term perspective and produces bureaucrats whose capacities gravitate toward immediate problems rather than the broader picture; and (3) a lack of both presidential leadership (because of Watergate and the flawed presidency of Jimmy Carter) and a foreign policy consensus (among Congress and governmental leaders as well as the general public) to provide a framework for dealing with the changing contours of the international landscape during the 1970s. The resulting drift in American policy, probably most dramatically clear in relations with the Soviet Union, was particularly evident regarding Asia in general and Japan in particular.

Consequently, to deal effectively with the fashioning of a new Asian policy, special measures seem warranted to mitigate the emotional, intellectual, and institutional inhibitions that focus on this subject. One way in which this might be done effectively is to appoint a special task force on Asian policy composed of individuals drawn primarily from the private sector. It is imperative that such a task force be accorded top priority in the administration's foreign policy agenda and be charged to provide recommendations dealing with the whole of Asia and explicitly linking economic and political-strategic considerations that match our long-term national interests in the region. Such an approach would balance the babel of voices from Congress, private interest groups, the various departments and agencies, the American public, and the maneuvers of the Asian governments themselves, which today inhibit the formulation of coherent and comprehensive guidelines for action. There are numerous models for organizing such an effort—the American Williams Commission and the British Royal Commissions, for example—but it should emanate directly from the White House, given the breadth of the charge to devise an Asian policy. Such an approach will meet at least in part the inevitable and recurrent complaint that is likely to be directed at every administration after America's withdrawal from Vietnam that there is no foreign policy. Moreover, by narrowing the scope to a specific region, the opportunities for constructive and concrete policy recommendations are more probable than an endeavor (increasingly the domain of presidential speech writers rather than foreign policy specialists) to find a new global formula about which to build a consensus for America's role in the world. Finally, one highly probable result of a comprehensive review of our Asian policy will be to underscore the pre-eminence of Japan economically, politically, and militarily in the United States' policy toward the Asian Pacific.

Japan: Old Myths and New Realities

The Japanese-American alliance stands as the major achievement of American policy toward Asia since World War II. However, the special international conditions, military and economic, on which the alliance rested have fundamentally changed during the past decade. The past can no longer be extended into the future, and there must be a reordering of bilateral relations on both the economic and military levels.

There have been recurrent problems in Japanese-American trade relations since the early 1970s, but these problems have become so acute during the past few years that they have begun to cast a shadow over the foundations of the alliance itself. The basic facts that have led to the current situation are well known but deserve restatement. Japan has surpassed all industrialized nations in the international marketplace during the past 25 years. The Japanese have also had a chronic and sizable bilateral trade surplus with the United States, and this has lately had a particularly serious impact on some sectors of the American economy. Moreover, American political, business, and labor leaders increasingly perceive the current pattern of relations as rooted in long-term structural features of the Japanese economy, which are unlikely to be altered without basic shifts in policy even if the trade balance fluctuates. Japan's success is seen largely as the result of a working relationship between the government and the business world, which is not possible in this country under existing laws and in that sense seems unfair. This perception (shared by many in Europe) has led an increasing number of industries and labor organizations previously committed to free trade to advocate quotas and retaliatory policies against Japanese products. This has not only placed American government leaders on the defensive but also provoked the Japanese to resist and to resent the efforts to blame them while America tries to solve its domestic economic inadequacies by using neomercantilist (supply-side) policies. Moreover, the Japanese are unlikely to fundamentally change their performance in the immediate future. Because of the long-term likelihood of continuing price rises in oil and other critical raw materials that Japan must import almost entirely, it is virtually essential for the Japanese to continue to run substantial trade surpluses in manufactured goods. Cast purely in economic terms, the Japanese are not likely to alter their own policies in large part because there is no real policy choice; compelling basic international conditions make an alteration of the past unacceptable.

While Japan continues to ride the crest of success in the international economy, the United States, the architect of and dominant force in that economy until the early 1970s, has seen its position diminish substantially both globally and in regard to Japan. Many purely economic factors underlie this decline, some governmental (inconsistent fiscal and monetary policies and the absence of an exports policy), some in the performance of the American private sector (comparatively low rates of saving, a decline in worker productivity), and some in the shifts in international power beyond U.S. control (higher growth rates by other societies, the rise in the price of oil). Although the economic conflicts with Japan are almost uniformly seen in economic terms, clearly the roots of these conflicts extend deeply into noneconomic considerations. Political, psychological, and cultural factors have exacerbated the economic issues and cannot be considered as separate from them. They include: the substantial costs of underwriting Japanese security; the tolerance of a fully protected and controlled Japanese economy for two decades while permitting access to the American market in part for political reasons (support for a noncommunist ally); the persistence of economic practices and policies that are legally and culturally outside of the American experience; and, above all, the frustrations related to the decline of the dollar and the United States in the global economy. These noneconomic factors corroborate a general mood of uncertainty and defensiveness now widespread in the United States; together with the level of Japanese success in which its per capita GNP now approximates the U.S. level, they magnify the specific economic problems that have appeared.

Past American economic policy toward Japan (and the world), which stressed the value of interdependence and the economic rationality of the marketplace, sought to separate politics and economics to the greatest possible extent. Paradoxically, this policy was ultimately dependent for its success on international political stability (Pax Americana) and strong domestic political leadership, or consensus. During the 1950s and 1960s, as aptly noted by Marina Whitman, the implementation of free trade policy required frequent subordination of our "short-term economic interests, narrowly conceived, to the long-term political and economic advantages of strengthened economies in other free world nations and a viable trading and monetary system linking those nations."[2]

As Japan graphically illustrates, the continuous tension from interdependence among the forces of the global economic market and the sovereignty of the nation-state in defining policy toward that market, has been and will continue to be relieved through acts of political will by the nations involved. Classical economic theory and official pronouncements of the Japanese government notwithstanding, politics and economics cannot be separated. There is a need for adjustment of economic differences within the context of a new political-strategic framework that will allow the Americans and Japanese to trade off security considerations and economic interests. To so deal with economic issues case by case without explicitly linking them to broader political-strategic concerns is to misread the basic dynamics of the international economy of the 1950s and 1960s and to assure maximum conflict between Japan and the United States in the 1980s and beyond.

Japanese-American security relations also rest on a set of international circumstances that have been radically changed during the past decade. Since 1945, Japan has either been occupied by American troops or been a defense satellite under a hegemonic alliance arrangement within which Japanese security interests were ultimately seen as identical with those of the United States. The current Mutual Security Treaty (with only modest changes) was negotiated by John Foster Dulles in the early 1950s when Japan was an impoverished, occupied country and the United States was seeking allies as the cold war was spreading to Asia. For almost three decades since the end of the occupation there has been effectively no strategic policy beyond the American alliance. The Self-Defense Force budgets are scarcely more than weapons procurement programs, and the mission of these forces is to augment the U.S. military in the unlikely event of a conventional Soviet attack on Japanese territory. Security is narrowly defined as territorial defense, nuclear weapons are not to be developed or even deployed in Japan (with deterrence provided by the U.S. nuclear system), no troops are to be sent abroad, and Japan is constitutionally banned from even participating in a collective self-defense arrangement such as NATO. Japanese leaders claim that the mood of pacifism fostered by the constitution that outlaws war makes it politically impossible to go much beyond current efforts, which effectively make Japan a security dropout in international affairs.

Faced with this frustrating situation, American officials have reacted in ways that minimize their capacity to shape Japanese policy. Instead of recognizing that the real need is to establish an appropriate new strategic role for Japan (in keeping with the behavior of every other major power in the world), the United States has instead engaged in sterile arguments about the percentage of the national budget that ought to be spent for defense. Rather than privately indicating a desire for Japan to devise a new defense policy, the United States has publicly criticized their failure to so act—thereby insulting the government and the individuals involved, with counterproductive results. Economic policy is not linked with defense concerns in the context of our broader alliance relationship; the issues are treated separately, thereby forgoing any graduated sanctions that could be imposed and maximizing the likelihood of bilateral conflict on the security issue. The result has been to limit American effectiveness in influencing Japan's security policy at a time when it is increasingly clear that Japan will probably have to play a security role in Asia.

Before turning to specific proposals regarding U.S. policy toward Japan, it is necessary to examine the impact of Japanese domestic politics on the defense issue. Does Japan have the capacity to make appropriate and realistic adjustments in security policy in light of the altered international environment? There are a number of constraints on policy leadership intrinsic to the process by which foreign policy is made. Fragmented structure of the ruling Liberal Democratic Party, the absence of a strong leader among the party elite, the popular support of pacifism, and the primacy of the economic ministries (and conversely the weakness of Japan's Self-Defense Agency) in the budget-making process combine to inhibit serious reconsideration of national security policy and virtually obviate long-term security planning.

Contrary to recent assertions that Japan provides the ideal model of a society capable of adjusting to challenges of the postindustrial world of the final decades of the twentieth century,[3] even a casual inspection of history since World War II shows that all major foreign policy decisions involving political-security issues provoked prolonged, often agonizing, conflict and debate. The decision-making process, dominated by a conservative party that is internally divided, tends to produce broker-style leaders adept at building a coalition within the Diet and developing consensus without. This leadership style is in keeping with traditional Japanese values and in effectively resolving such issues as the rate of economic growth that have calculable costs. However, it is not suited to the bold, personal leadership that has characterized those nations that have actively participated in international politics in recent years—the United States, France, China, India, Israel, and the Soviet Union, for example. The resulting slow, almost immobile process of decision making in regard to controversial political and security issues in foreign policy will continue to inhibit Japan as a participant in the swiftly changing world of international politics and make it probable that the timing and substance of security policy will be essentially dictated by the drift of international events, not by decisions of politicians in Tokyo. Accordingly, this provides wide latitude for the United States to shape the direction of Japanese policy.

Another distinctive feature of the Japanese approach to the issues of defense and bilateral relations with the United States is an emotionalism that encourages extreme reactions. For this, the United States, and particularly the American occupation of Japan, bear much of the responsibility. Article IX of Japan's constitution renouncing war "as a sovereign right of the nation and the threat or use of force in settling international disputes" has become a moral symbol from which Japanese policy has not gravitated very far.[4] The no-war clause was a radical statement, reflecting an idealism strongly felt in the years after World War II and part of the missionary cast of MacArthur's approach to the Japanese people. It gave legal sanctity and symbolic dignity to pacifism and renounced what is acknowledged as the elemental requisite for a state's participation in international politics. In consequence, the various conservative governments have operated in a pacifist milieu and have been continuously on the defensive in the sporadic efforts to develop a security policy. Above all, the idealism embodied in Article IX has given all matters of defense a peculiarly moral cast and drawn the questions of security deeply into the issue of constitutional revision and into the basic attitudes held by individuals toward the foundation of the postwar political order. Moreover, throughout most of the past three decades, the United States has served as kind of a political-cultural stepfather to Japan, a relationship that was indeed special from the Japanese perspective and that has added another emotional overlay to the question of the bilateral alliance. This, too, inhibits easy change in foreign policy.

Prolonged withdrawal from international politics and insulation from direct military threats from abroad (made possible by projection of American power into Asia through the mid-1970s under a hegemonic alliance arrangement) has led to a distorted security debate within Japan. Among Japanese intellectuals, specialists, and political parties, the debate over security is shaped almost entirely by internal considerations. The result has been an unrealistic debate about issues such as "disarmed neutralism," the legality of the armed forces, and the separation of politics and economics—issues free from any serious reference to the world in which Japan lives. Normally, a nation's strategic policy reflects a dynamic balance between internal and international considerations, but in postwar Japan this relationship has been disrupted. A gap has developed between international realities and the willingness and capacity of the Japanese to come to grips with them. This underlays the surprising and emotional reaction within Japan over the meaning of the word *alliance* in the 1981 joint communiqué of President Reagan and Prime Minister Zenko Suzuki. In the process through which Japan comes to have a more normal and responsible security policy, other difficult adjustments can be expected between the nature of the domestic political debate and international realities, as well as further conflicts with the United States.

Accordingly, there are three essential ways in which Japanese domestic politics impinge on foreign policy: (1) there is a serious gap between the focus of the security debate within Japan and contemporary international realities, (2) there is a diffuse and immobile foreign policymaking process that projects Japanese domestic politics (particularly conservative *habatsu*, or fractional, politics) deeply into consideration of major issues, and (3) there is an emotional and moral overlay to policies relating to defense and the United States that inhibits the formulation of pragmatic realistic policies.

Recently, security policy has surfaced as a major issue in Japanese politics and has been caught up in the inter- and intraparty maneuvering in ways that add a new dimension to the problem. As the matter of defense has become ensnared in domestic politics, it has become clear that the public mood on this issue has tilted sharply toward a more nationalist and anti-American posture than was even conjectured a few years ago. (For example, a majority of the ruling party leans toward revising the constitution.) Accordingly, although there is considerable latitude for the United States to shape the direction of Japanese security policy because of the static nature of the decision-making process, Washington must now pay more scrupulous attention to the dynamics of Japanese politics than at any time since the end of the occupation.

Japan, not China, should be the focal point of American policy toward Asia. The extreme uncertainty regarding the stability of Chinese domestic politics, the enormous problems of economic growth in an overpopulated, poor country with a highly politicized populace, the chasm of differences separating an essentially democratic Japan from a communist China, and the volatility and indeterminacy of the belligerent Sino-Soviet confrontation combine to make it extremely risky to maintain anything but cordial, limited contacts with Beijing. Since we have never really clarified our common security interests with China except to speak loosely of our quasi-ally and to transfer some military technology, America's policy toward China must be more specifically defined within the context of a broader, coherent Asian policy. This lack of clarity in America's China policy maximizes the capacity of the Chinese for policy maneuvers, inhibits our policy options with Japan, and makes us hostage to political developments in China that we barely comprehend, far less control. Indeed, by making China the cornerstone of our Asian policy we sacrifice our credibility toward other parts of Asia and gain only peripheral influence on the Sino-Soviet confrontation, which has a momentum of its own.

Can the Japanese-American security relationship be constructively redefined? What are the incentives for doing so? From a military perspective there are three critical problems in northeast Asia that could affect in basic ways the American-Japanese relationship: the continuing confrontation on the Korean peninsula, the Sino-Soviet conflict, and the Soviet-American military balance. Nevertheless, without a clearer and more coherent set of priorities, the prospect is that our security policy toward Japan will change only in ad hoc fashion after one of these issues erupts into a crisis. In the past, the United States has dealt in a direct and discrete way with security issues in this region and only peripherally involved the Japanese. However appropriate this pattern of action was to the era of containment and an activist military posture in Asia, the needs for the future are different, both because of the new configuration of power in the region and the necessity of broadening the definition of security to deal with economic and political, as well as military, considerations.

One of the new realities of international affairs in northeast Asia with which American policy must deal is the drift of Japanese relations with China and the Soviet Union. Until quite recently, Japanese dependence on the American security commitment (that is, the Mutual Security Treaty) was supplemented by a policy of equidistance between China and the Soviet Union. This has now changed and Japan currently leans toward China. The Sino-Japanese Treaty of Friendship and Amity signed in 1978 contained a clearly anti-Soviet clause deploring hegemonism of any power in Asia. Even more important, the Japanese have plunged into trade, loan, and technical assistance agreements with Beijing that completely overshadow those that any nation has taken or is likely to take. This extensive economic involvement is colored by attitudes of cultural and racial affinity and, in some circles in Japan, by a romantic approach even exceeding that evident in American policy toward China. The scope and intensity of this involvement have, if nothing else, drawn Japan more fully into the tumultuous stream of Chinese politics and at an equal rate into northeast Asian international relations. Beyond dissociating themselves from Deng Xiaoping's urgings for a China-Japan-United States alliance, Japan has yet to confront fully the problem of deeper entanglement with China. American leaders similarly have merely waxed euphoric about the enhanced prospects for stability, now that Japan and China have good relations with each other and with the United States, without due consideration for the past pattern of volatile change in China. Whether American and Japanese interests in China coincide and whether broadened contacts with Beijing will have a salutary effect on relations between Tokyo and Washington are problematical issues central to our future security role in the region.

Japan should prove extremely valuable in limiting Soviet influence in Asia. Soviet-Japanese relations, historically bad, have turned even worse as relations between Japan and China have improved. The Soviet failure to return the four islands north of Hokkaido and the recent deployment of troops on the islands, the heavy-handed way in which Moscow imposed the 200-mile fishing limit, and the expansion of the Soviet fleet in the Pacific have all fed this animosity. Now, as previously noted, the Soviet Union is seen as the main security threat to Japan.

Soviet-Japanese economic relations are likely to continue to expand, but they are unlikely to reach proportions envisioned by those who see Siberia (rather than China) as the place where Japanese capital and technology will develop Soviet resources to tilt significantly the geopolitical balance in this part of the world. The costs of developing Siberian resources are so huge that a long-term multinational effort seems necessary to make the enterprise commercially feasible on a grand scale. The Japanese are not likely to assume singlehandedly the political and economic risks of such an endeavor. Moreover, the size and nature of many resources in Siberia remain matters of conjecture despite the enormous investments the Soviets have made. Certainly the exploitable supplies of oil and gas are still matters of dispute and are not likely to attract massive Japanese investments in the near future. Although the level of economic involvement by Japan in Siberian development is unlikely to reach a level of strategic importance, bilateral trade—essentially the resources of the Maritime Territory and Siberia and Japanese equipment to develop these resources—is likely to grow at the steady rate of the past two decades. (Bilateral trade has now reached roughly $5 billion.) However, Soviet-Japanese economic relations will remain subordinate to political-security considerations, thereby leaving considerable room for flexibility in American policy.

To continue its highly successful alliance with Japan, the United States must clarify and link its own strategic and economic objectives toward northeast Asia. On the one hand, the Japanese must truly be treated as a partner in diplomatic actions regarding China, Korea, and other parts of northeast Asia. At the same time, it is neither reasonable nor domestically viable for the United States virtually to underwrite Japan's security while running a massive and seemingly chronic bilateral trade deficit. The risks of a serious negative reaction within the United States to the reluctance of Tokyo to play an expanded role in defense are particularly high since the Japanese alliance does not rest on the deep-seated cultural and political ties that link America to Europe. This places a special burden on American political leaders to devise an acceptable new policy. Without decisive leadership from the United States, Japanese security policy will emerge not from diplomatic calculation but from the crosscurrents of international events and the inherently nationalist pull of domestic politics in both countries. The most important and long-standing diplomatic achievement of the United States in Asia should not be permitted to wither through inertia or ineptness.

If Japan is to be brought into a new alliance with the United States with expanded security responsibilities as the cornerstone of our Asian policy, it is essential that economic and political issues be explicitly linked. What specifically this new relationship would entail is best left to diplomatic negotiation. However, it is necessary to look beyond the NATO model (recommended by one recent study) so that mutual security interests of the United States and Japan regarding such questions as access to oil and raw materials in the Third World and nuclear proliferation can be more effectively handled. International events and American domestic politics require that the United States establish a new realistic policy toward Asia and Japan. If the government fails to heed this imperative, the United States will surely forfeit its leadership role in the Pacific, and the United States' future in the region will be defined by the drift of circumstance. Such a turn of events is unnecessary and unacceptable. Similarly, to stress China as the cornerstone of our policy toward Asia and to attempt to bring Japan into a political-strategic arrangement focused on further involvement on the Asiatic mainland would run risks intrinsically high and certainly unacceptable to Tokyo. Japan is now a greater industrial power than Russia, and it holds a critical place among the noncommunist Asian nations with the most rapidly growing economies in the world. Surely a strategy in which Japan and the United States work together to devise a new political, military, and economic partnership focused on developing these societies is the most attractive and appropriate route for U.S. policy in Asia.

Notes

1. Ezra Vogel, *Japan as Number One: Lessons for America* (Cambridge, Mass.: University Press, 1979).

2. Marina V. N. Whitman, "Leadership Without Hegemony: Our Role in the World Economy," *Foreign Policy* 20 (1975): 140.

3. Vogel, *Japan as Number One*.

4. For Japanese constitution, see Robert E. Ward, *Japan's Political System*, 2d ed. (Englewood Cliffs, N.J.: Prentice-Hall, 1978). See appendix, pp. 229–43.

6 | THE U.S. POSITION IN ASIA AND THE PACIFIC: THE RELEVANCE OF AUSTRALIA AND NEW ZEALAND

Henry S. Albinski

American resources are globally dispersed and finite. Appropriate diplomatic, economic, and defense policies toward particular Asian-Pacific states will most likely be accepted and effective if coupled with efforts by others. In some instances, for reasons of tradition, location, or sheer resource differential, the United States' access to Asia will be more difficult than that of others who are willing and able to serve in complementary roles. It is in this sense and context that Australia's and New Zealand's benefits to U.S. objectives can be appraised.

The relevance of Australia and New Zealand to the fulfillment of foreseeable U.S. security objectives in Asia and the Pacific is likely to be considerable. Singly or within the framework of the Australia–New Zealand–United States (ANZUS) treaty alliance, Australia and New Zealand are capable of contributing substantially more than might outwardly be assumed from two middle-sized powers, located on the periphery of the Asian Pacific basin. In part because it will be relying on Australian and New Zealand assets, the United States must approach its relationship with them in proportion, mindful of the constraints under which they operate and sensitive to points of difference that, on balance, need not disturb the high quality of the partnership.

The ANZUS Relationship

Unlike so many of the nations or clusters of nations in the Pacific Ocean, Australia and New Zealand will not foreseeably require that the United

States expend its energies and resources to contain, stabilize, placate, defend, or resuscitate them. Instead, with only a slight margin of uncertainty, and at small trade-off cost, the United States will be able to benefit from Australian and New Zealand contributions relative to the achievement of American purposes within the greater region.

What these assets represent, and how and why they somehow might become tempered, needs to be spelled out in some detail. The argument can be taken in two, related parts. The first bears on the value to the United States of the tone, complement, and cohesiveness of its Australian, New Zealand, and ANZUS alliance relationships. The second is reflected in Australia's and New Zealand's demonstrated or prospective capabilities to pursue policies that support U.S. objectives.

It is of primary importance that the quality of their relationship is in considerable measure traceable to the similarity of American, Australian, and New Zealand interpretations of world and regional developments and the means by which to respond. This includes views about the interregional significance of rivalry between great powers, the ascription of mischievous motives to the USSR, and the need to appreciate the varieties and sensibilities of individual and regionally associated states that are not in direct line of First and Second World conflicts, as within the ASEAN community and in the South Pacific. Both Australia and New Zealand place a high premium on an effective and credible American presence in the region. Both feel that the United States should be encouraged and supported. This, they feel, adds to the weight of the overall security-political effort and ameliorates American feelings of isolation and burden. ANZUS unites and further legitimizes regional security efforts. It serves as example to others and provides for their foreseeable security requirements.

These are the views of the incumbent, Malcolm Fraser Liberal–National Country Party government in Australia and the Robert Muldoon National Party government in New Zealand. But, as will be illustrated later, these views are more conditionally held by the opposition Labor parties in the two countries, which have in recent times been much more often out of power rather than in power. Since 1949, the Australian Labor Party (ALP) has governed only from 1972 to 1975 and the New Zealand Labour Party only during 1957 to 1960 and 1972 to 1975. Additionally, although the Labor oppositions and other critics have often berated non-Labor governments for being too dependent on or even servile toward the United States, the United States has by trial and error learned reasonably well to maintain satisfactory communication with the alternative government parties.

To illustrate, in 1979 the outgoing U.S. ambassador to Wellington, Armistead Selden, publicly rebuked the New Zealand Labour Party for its position on barring visits by American nuclear powered vessels (NPVs). The Department of State endorsed Selden's conclusions, but felt that political circumstances were not propitious for this position to be ventilated in this manner. Not only was Labour leader W. E. Rowling visiting Washington at the time but also the nuclear accident at Three Mile Island had just occurred, and Selden's proposed remarks could produce "a short-term setback" for the cause of NPV access to New Zealand.[1] The case was thereafter put to the Labour Party, but with greater tact. In Australia, after some initial difficulties between Prime Minister Gough Whitlam's Australian Labor Party government and the United States, U.S. Ambassador Marshall Green openly questioned the group tendencies of previous, non-Labor parties toward wholehearted embrace of the United States: "Too rigid relations can snap in the winds of controversy; if it's flexible, it bends with the wind. I think that this is a more resilient, healthy, enduring relationship that we have today."[2]

In both countries, moreover, public sentiment supports the American connection and generally the current political perceptions in Canberra and Wellington. This is especially true in Australia. A 1978 poll disclosed that four of five respondents believed that Australia's security would continue to depend on the United States in the 1980s. The same proportion had confidence that the United States would deal wisely with world problems and would assist Australia if it were threatened. Overall, a very considerable "reservoir of goodwill" toward the United States was detected.[3] In late 1979, 47 percent of Australians felt that American power in the world would increase, while only 18 percent believed that it would decline. Among twenty nations polled, Australia ranked third (after the United States and the Philippines) in anticipating a rise in American power. In the same series of polls, Australia placed second (after the United States) in anticipating a rise in Soviet power.[4] After the invasion of Afghanistan, Australians felt threatened by the Soviet Union,[5] and expressed approval of increased Australian defense spending.[6]

Comparable New Zealand survey data are not available. In degree, however, New Zealanders regard themselves as less centrally placed, less vulnerable, and less threatened by great or intermediate powers than Australians do. New Zealanders also feel that they can do less about what happens overseas, with the special exception of the neighboring South Pacific community. For the moment, the prescriptive point is that, in the interest of the ANZUS alliance and in its own interest, the United States should exercise self-discipline toward a small and sensitive ally. It must also frequently remind itself that, while similar, Australia and New Zealand are not identical, and that New Zealanders of all party persuasions are offended when they feel that they are being treated as an extension of Australia and of Australians.

In addition, it does not follow that, apart from opposition party and other New Zealand and Australian group reservations about following the United States too closely, non-Labor governments in the two countries routinely imitate the United States or wait for signals from Washington. From the standpoint of American self-interest, this by no means constitutes a serious problem and, in some respects, is an asset. Practices that depart from, but rarely are discordant with, U.S. preferences and objectives lessen the susceptibility of pro-American Australian and New Zealand governments to charges of servitude at their own, national expense. In the idiom of the United States' Guam doctrine, which encouraged regional self-reliance and its subsequent and anticipated variants, more independently conceived and self-reliant Australian and New Zealand regional policies are welcome. We will, moreover, show that in certain instances where Australia and New Zealand have taken exception to American diplomacy or to defense measures, they have done so without fanfare and acrimony, and their positions could be construed as generally being productive, not counterproductive, toward U.S. interests.

This leads more directly to an assessment of the present and prospective value to the United States to uphold the ANZUS treaty alliance that binds the three states. ANZUS is an established, intimate, highly utilitarian alliance among three, charter members that substantially share perceptions of international conflict and of regional security management. Unlike the Central Treaty Organization (CENTO) or the Southeast Asia Treaty Organization (SEATO), ANZUS has never been subjected to membership erosion, or to the fissiparousness symptomatic of collections of far-flung nations governed by disparate regimes. Indeed, all three partners have to date resisted the enlargement of ANZUS. In the past few years the Cook Islands have inquired about ANZUS membership, Papua New Guinea has toyed with associate membership, and the Solomons have broached the idea of observer status at ANZUS council meetings. Some academic and official thought has been given to adding Japan. Among the reasons against enlargement has been the conviction that the cohesion, intimacy, and worth of the alliance would be diluted. Short of being encouraged to consider affiliation with ANZUS, however, Japan has in various ways widened its defense contacts with Australia and New Zealand, as well as with the United States. Its participation in the 1980 Rim of the Pacific (RIMPAC) exercises and its early indication of willingness to participate again in 1982 were politically facilitated because of RIMPAC's multinational character; it includes Australia, New Zealand, and Canada. Japan's 1981 promise to extend the radius of air and naval patrols by the Self-Defense Force can in degree enable the United States, with some Australian assistance, to focus surveillance more on the southwest quadrant of the Pacific, a requirement heightened by Soviet access to Vietnamese facilities.

Given ANZUS's longevity, tightness, and otherwise sound reputation, neglect or denigration of it would strain America's credibility as a security guarantor, and its position and leverage in the Asian Pacific basin would be undercut. In the anticipated shifting circumstances of the coming decade and beyond, this in turn could encourage opportunistic and perhaps unmanageable maneuvers by friends and antagonists alike. The governing principle was summarized during the closing months of the Ford administration: "A withdrawal of the United States from the Western Pacific—from any part of our chain of bases that do have interrelation in military terms, that are not discrete entities—would be perceived as a collapse of American interests. This would seriously affect what the Japanese think about our commitment there and the Koreans and, for that matter, our allies in the ANZUS Pact."[7]

Overall, however, and in keeping with American security objectives in Asia and the Pacific, the prospects are that the ANZUS alliance will continue and probably prosper. One reason lies in the compatibility of views and assessments on the part of the members. Another reason, somewhat less obvious but perhaps no less significant, lies in the lack of onerous American obligations toward Australia and New Zealand. These are stable societies with stable political systems. Unlike some regional states—for instance, Malaysia and the Philippines— they are not distracted by communal tensions or internal insurgencies. Their political and civil liberties conduct does not condemn them in the eyes of the international community in ways that could complicate close security relations with the United States. Greater assertiveness among Australian Aborigines and New Zealand Maoris does not militate against this conclusion. Australia, with an earlier history of a racially exclusionist migration policy, has, on a basis of per capita population, admitted more Indochinese refugees than any other country in the world.

In other ways as well, Australia and New Zealand have avoided becoming diplomatic burdens or embarrassments to the United States. Neither has a nuclear capability or is likely to seek one. Both are known for their strong antiproliferation and antinuclear-testing spokesmanship. Unlike Indonesia's situation in East Timor, neither has unsatisfied or contentious international claims nor a burdensome colonial record.

The ANZUS treaty refers to possible assistance by members to other signatories, in accordance with constitutional processes, in the event of "an armed attack on the metropolitan territory of any of the Parties, on its armed forces, public vessels or aircraft in the Pacific." In the 1950s, New Zealand and Australia did not feel obligated to support the United States to defend Taiwan and its offshore islands. In the 1960s, the United States was averse to promising support for its partners against Indonesia during confrontation. But neither dispute escalated. Not then, or in other instances, has ANZUS really come close to being tested. The United States has therefore not had to resolve dilemmas associated with upholding or reneging on actual or assumed security obligations toward Australia and New Zealand. Nor has it or is it likely to make investments of economic or security assistance, or of protective forces on behalf of Australia and New Zealand. When the United States has obtained access to Australia or New Zealand for various defense-related facilities, no quid pro quo has been extracted by the host countries.

Australia and New Zealand have, to be sure, often taken exception to American economic policies and have pressed their case forcefully. This has ranged from U.S. meat quotas to tariffs and multilateral trade negotiations and from civil aviation to the impact on New Zealand and Australia of extraterritorial features of American law. The United States has, however, been gratified that, even under Labor governments, these economic disputes have not been allowed to encroach upon and undermine political and security relations. It is even arguable that present and prospective American security interests stand to benefit from the firm and often public economic representations made by Australia and New Zealand. Even more in this economic context than previously suggested, when they deviate from the United States in their political or defense behavior, the non-Labor governments in Australia and New Zealand are thereby less vulnerable to imputations that they comprehensively and humbly give way to Washington without regard for Australian or New Zealand honor or interests.

The United States has on occasion been persuaded to make conciliatory gestures toward Australia and New Zealand on matters of importance to them, in recognition of their political steadfastness and defense value. But such concessions should be interpreted as small tokens exchanged for major alliance returns. Almost immediately following the Soviet intrusion in Afghanistan, Fraser paid two successful and constructive visits to Carter. In part because of Prime Minister Fraser's reputation as a promoter of Australian economic causes, the contacts with President Carter were kept uncluttered by the Australians with issues extraneous to security themes. It was noticed and appreciated in Washington that the gravity of Afghanistan was not debased. Because of Australia's highly supportive position on Afghanistan, Indian Ocean security, and related matters, the Department of State found it easier in the following months to represent various Australian economic interests before Congress and executive departments. This included a Department of Justice submission that urged U.S. courts to weigh the principle of international comity in a multibillion-dollar Westinghouse civil litigation that affected several Australian uranium supplier defendants.

Nor has it been nor should it in the future be difficult for the United States to make allowances for New Zealand's economic circumstances. New Zealand's economy is smaller and markedly weaker than Australia's, and it is especially sensitive to foreign exchange pressures. In early 1980, the United States did not expect and did not get as much from New Zealand as it did from Australia in the form of economic sanctions against the Soviet Union in the aftermath of Afghanistan, in large measure because it appreciated the value to New Zealand of its trade balance surplus with the Soviets. In 1977, New Zealand was prepared to grant the Soviet Union fishing privileges. Fraser thought that this could become a Soviet wedge into the South Pacific and appealed to Carter. Here too the United States appreciated New Zealand's economic constraints. It also felt that surveillance capabilities were sufficient to monitor Soviet behavior. It refused to be drawn into the dispute; Richard Holbrooke explained that the United States "was not going to go around telling New Zealand what it should or should not do" and that such an intervention would not promote the common interests of ANZUS.[8] Australia withdrew its complaint, and there were no untoward reverberations.

The incident also served to underscore that ANZUS's compactness and the compatibility of its partners have minimized onerous American responsibilities to act as a mediator or manager of intra-alliance disputes affecting Australia and New Zealand. These two countries have their share of bilateral differences, but they are not fundamental and have not degraded security relations between them. The United States has not had to cater to disputatious partners in the way it has had to deal with Greece and Turkey in NATO. In part because the two nations have historically operated along complementary lines, the alliance's acceptance in New Zealand could weaken simply if a Labour government there felt that Australia had gone overboard on promoting tough-mindedness on various security issues.

One other, critical variable serves to relieve the United States of unwelcome burdens, and in so doing hardens the alliance's integrity. Australia and New Zealand are insular countries, steady and stable. They are geographically off the Asian center stage, do not face threatening neighbors, and have no heavily armed state anywhere close to their shores. They are therefore not prospectively susceptible to direct threat or interdiction. Much of the official thinking in all the ANZUS capitals assumes that Australia and New Zealand do not, in their own right, face serious security threats. Apart from some low-level threat scenarios, whatever their plausibility, Australia's and New Zealand's essential security is believed to depend on broader regional and even global events outside their immediate strategic environment. As in past decades, therefore, the United States is unlikely to have its ANZUS treaty obligations and credit severely tested or its resources diverted from elsewhere in the Asian Pacific region.

Although the United States is not lumbered by ANZUS treaty obligations, there has been a gradual, informal, but useful accretion of the alliance's nominal, geographical reach. There have been efforts by non-Labor governments in Canberra and Wellington to engage and maintain American interest, presence, and credibility over a broad arc stretching from Oceania to the Indian Ocean. But this has not constituted an entrapment of the United States, which has not been averse to following this course. In this context, the United States has increasingly accepted, even welcomed, some form of de facto, pan-ANZUS association or canopy for its activities. At Australian urging, the 1977 ANZUS council communiqué asserted that any Soviet-American arms limitation agreement in the Indian Ocean "must be balanced in its effects and consistent with the security interests of the ANZUS partners."[9] Later that year, Cyrus Vance, in an open letter to Australian Foreign Minister Andrew Peacock, wrote that such an agreement "will not in any way qualify or derogate from the United States' commitment to Australia or limit our freedom to act in implementing our commitment under the ANZUS treaty"; he added that the Soviets had been so advised and specified that joint exercises in the Indian Ocean under ANZUS aegis would not be affected.[10] A similar trend has developed in another regional setting. By 1978, Lester Wolff, chairman of the House Subcommittee on Asian and Pacific Affairs, told his hosts in Papua New Guinea that, through ANZUS, American concern extended to it.[11] Holbrooke, on his part, testified before Congress that because the South Pacific was of special importance to Australia and New Zealand—two of America's staunchest allies—"we do take this [ANZUS] connection into account."[12] Replying to a question during his confirmation hearings, Gen. Alexander Haig stepped beyond conventional praise of ANZUS, stressing in particular Australian and New Zealand security contributions within a wide, Asian Pacific radius.[13]

A generous interpretation of alliance coverage or joint efforts by the partners will likely continue to invest U.S. security policies with broader legitimacy. An elastic rather than narrowly construed ANZUS coverage also helps to husband Australian and New Zealand territorial, military, and diplomatic resources.

Australia's and New Zealand's Contributions to U.S. Security Objectives

We now assess Australia's and New Zealand's particular contributions to present or prospective U.S. security objectives. Three such categories of benefits will be identified. The first deals with benefits available to the United States by utilizing or operating in conjunction with Australian and New Zealand facilities and forces. The second refers to the manner in which benefits accrue to the United States when New Zealand and Australian defense efforts are exerted essentially separately from the United States. The third category focuses on how, through a combination of diplomatic, economic, and defense means, Australia and New Zealand can help to shape regional developments supportive of general, short- or long-term U.S. regional objectives.

Australia and New Zealand, but especially the former because of its size and location, house significant American astronomical, communications, navigational, and space-tracking facilities. These are either under joint management with the host country or entirely under host country operation. A number of these, either in place or scheduled to be built, such as the Mt. John and Transit Circle observatory facilities in New Zealand and the Omega navigational and Tranet tracking stations in Australia, operate with various degrees of civilian and military applications. These facilities and other, specifically defense-related but nonbase installations, notably in Australia, have interregional coverage, including into the Indian Ocean, where sustained American attention will almost surely continue. The North-West Cape naval communication station at Exmouth Gulf, Western Australia, has a high capability for shore-to-ship message traffic and for very low frequency communication with submerged craft. It is linked to other stations, including Diego Garcia and San Miguel in the Philippines, as part of a global network. The space-tracking and communications facilities at Pine Gap and at Nurrungar, in the interior of Australia, command, control, receive, process, and transmit data from satellites on a real-time basis, applicable to surveillance, deterrence, and inferentially, to fighting capabilities. The United States has reportedly, with Australia's assistance, strung a sophisticated, seabed sensor system for antisubmarine warfare in the southeastern portion of the Indian Ocean.

These facilities and activities have not been free of public controversy within Australia and New Zealand. To date, however, the United States can feel reasonably confident that these strategic assets will not be compromised. Various groups in the host countries have alleged that such facilities can create undesirable and otherwise avoidable entanglement in American adventures and that they compound the risk of Soviet interdiction against them. It is not, however, the standing policy of the major opposition parties in either country to close down or otherwise degrade the American facilities. In Australia, where U.S. facilities are especially prominent and strategically significant, the ALP leadership has defended Pine Gap and Nurrungar in particular on grounds of their role in a global system of deterrence and of verification of strategic arms limitation agreements. However, its public position is that Australia should acquire access to and potentially veto power over the especially combat-related, U.S. message traffic transmitted through the North-West Cape station.[14]

The United States opposes Labor's position on North-West Cape signals, but has come around to the view that general disclosure about the interior facilities is desirable, in part because doing so would make them, and the U.S. presence generally, more palatable to Australian opinion, to Labor particularly. It has been the Australian government itself that has persisted in shielding what by now are—in general terms—nonsecrets. Not wishing to breach good form with an ally, the United States has not proceeded to make unilateral disclosures. As a matter of prescription, however, the United States should be scrupulously attentive to the sensibilities of partners who are part of an asymmetrical alliance. Failure to do so, even with non-Labor governments in charge in Canberra and Wellington, can magnify suspicions of the United States and impede normally relaxed relations. Hence, in 1978, it came to light in Australia that the United States had prepared to let contracts for a new terminal at the North-West Cape signal station. Australian officials had been aware of the plans, but had not advised politically responsible persons. The United States felt that since no new capabilities were inherent in the installation of the equipment and Australian officials had been consulted and had approved, nothing else was needed. But it was a politically awkward episode for all concerned. ALP leader William Hayden remarked in a radio interview that the lack of proper consultation by the United States "places an unreasonable and undesirable strain on that relationship." Speaking on the same program, Defense Minister D. J. Killen averred that Australia "will not be taken for granted." Although Australia had not actually been kept in the dark, it had not been "treated with the proper courtesy."[15] He also insisted that if the United States wished to install a new terminal, it would need to file a formal request.[16] This was done, and in turn approved by the government.

One moral of this incident is that keen sensitivity toward its allies is a small price for the United States to pay for the value of the facilities and other assets provided by Australia and New Zealand. Some disappointment, and patience, may also need to be borne. For instance, protest groups and some sectors of the trade union movements in both countries have variously, but never decisively, created some difficulties related to security for the United States. In the late 1960s, for example, the United States first explored both New Zealand and Australia as sites for locating an Omega navigational station. New Zealand was ostensibly rejected for technical reasons. But the most reliable evidence is that, faced with considerable anti-Omega public feeling, the National Party government advised that it would be politically imprudent to select a New Zealand site. The United States then turned to Australia. A decision there to accept a station languished under the Labor government. The succeeding Labor–National Country Party government agreed to it, despite some protests by trade unions and others that the station would constitute another American base on Australian soil. Construction eventually got under way, but in 1980 was interrupted and remained interrupted for ten months because of a bitter jurisdictional dispute between two unions about which was entitled to the job; the United States approached the point of considering pulling the project out.

To date, the United States has not established any base facilities in either Australia or New Zealand, apart from the essentially nonmilitary Antarctic support operations conducted from Christchurch by United States services. American aircraft do, however, occasionally transit through Australia's Cocos Islands during Indian Ocean deployments. Port visits by major U.S. ships and submarines to Western Australia are commonplace, less frequent elsewhere in Australia, and even rarer in New Zealand. A more elaborate American naval presence in Western Australia, with options including task force home ports, is under consideration. Substantial time and funds would be required to upgrade the existing Royal Australian Navy base at Cockburn Sound if a major U.S. presence were favored, and the site has other drawbacks. But, in part either as a complement to Philippine bases or as a hedge against their possible untenability, Australia's offer of Cockburn Sound widens American strategic options in one of the region's most stable and politically friendly nations.

The ALP has not taken strong exception to visits by vessels that are nuclear powered or may be carrying nuclear weapons. But, again for reasons of Australian avoidance of entanglement or of risks of Soviet attack or hostage taking, it has objected to the notion of prospective U.S. home ports or other major privileges at Cockburn Sound and especially to vessels with nuclear arms being stationed there. It has also, for similar reasons underscored by arguments about Australian sovereignty, reproached the agreement with America to stage B-52 flights through Darwin as not providing absolute Australian authority to ban such aircraft were they to carry nuclear weapons.[17]

The B-52 issue illuminates the assets for regional security made available to the United States by Australia and also serves as a needed reminder that Australian or New Zealand compliance with American wishes cannot be expected automatically, simply, and unconditionally. Once again, therefore, perspective and some patience will be called for if the United States is to realize maximum substantive benefit from its partners at minimum political cost.

In 1980 the United States took up an Australian invitation to transit Guam-based B-52s through Australia, with Darwin becoming the chosen site. Negotiations were completed shortly after the Reagan administration took office. The Australian government did not meekly accept an American formula. It generally shared its principal concerns with the Australian public, and otherwise assumed a posture that was independently Australian as well as supportive of the United States, ANZUS, and noncommunist security interests at large. Part of this approach was inspired by a wish to educate and win over the bulk of the Australian public and, as far as possible, to neutralize ALP and other skeptical opinion, not only about the B-52s but also regarding an alliance that in appearance as well as fact needed to be grounded more on partnership than on subservience. Given its need to maintain public political support for its facilities in Australia, the United States should not be unsympathetic toward such positions on the part of a friendly government.

There were two, related areas in which the United States found accommodation necessary. The first, and less publicized, was Australia's desire that B-52s transiting through the country to the Indian Ocean do so on missions outwardly connected with containing the Soviets, especially in response to the Soviet presence in Afghanistan. Australia settled on an understanding that the aircraft were aimed at containing a Soviet regional threat generally. Neither in fact nor in appearance did Australia want B-52 deployments directed at indigenous Persian Gulf and Middle Eastern disputes. In part, it wished to preserve its own political and commercial reputation in the region. In part, it wished to avoid a negative reception among Asian Pacific-basin nations with whom it has cultivated and will likely continue to cultivate political and defense relations that sustain American as well as Australian interests. The B-52s will foreseeably be deployed on unarmed training and surveillance missions and will provide a demonstration of U.S. force projection capabilities and of resolve for an alliance. Such objectives, we have suggested, will be a central feature of the United States position in the Indo-Pacific region in the context of counteracting Soviet power.

In the second place, to make the B-52 deployments more politically palatable, the Fraser government pressed for a formula that would give Australia knowledge of and technically veto power over any future armed flights. But the United States does not in specific instances confirm or deny, even with allies, that a system is armed with nuclear weapons. The language of the agreement, together with informal understandings, suggests that both sides have been able to preserve their basic requirements.[18]

It must be conceded that nuclear-related issues in New Zealand set potentially nettlesome problems for regional American security interests. As indicated, the New Zealand Labour Party is on balance somewhat more critical of the U.S. connection than is its Australian counterpart. Although the party's position is not altogether free of ambiguity, it has in sum been disquieting to the United States. The party opposes NPV visits to New Zealand, as well as transit rights for naval forces or aircraft armed with nuclear weapons. The professed rationale, which refers to New Zealand's own safety and protection from attack or entanglement, is at root conceived as an extension of the party's wish to foster a nuclear-free zone in the South Pacific.[19] Moreover, although American NPV visits to New Zealand ports have been far less frequent than to Australia, they have at times been seriously obstructed by protesters. In 1979, the port of Wellington was closed for nearly a week because of disturbances associated with the visit of an American NPV.

The frequently expressed U.S. position, backed by the National Party government, is that NPV port calls create no safety hazards. NPV's represent some 40 percent of major American combatant units and are especially useful in operating across the great distances found in the Pacific. They require clear passage in and around New Zealand, for both operational and alliance-nurturing reasons. A ban on nuclear-armed craft could mean no visits at all, given the principle of neither confirmation nor denial.[20]

In 1980, the New Zealand Labour Party passed a technically nonbinding resolution favoring New Zealand's withdrawal from ANZUS.[21] Rowling, on his part, has not advocated this step. Instead, he has argued for a greater nonmilitary orientation within ANZUS. He has claimed that the treaty as such does not obligate New Zealand to accept naval or air visits from partners in the alliance. In his view, denial of such visits would not undermine the treaty. At all events, the future of U.S.–New Zealand relations and the status of ANZUS would for Rowling and a number of his political associates substantially depend on American attitudes toward the nuclear question.[22]

There is another potential dimension to the problem, extending beyond nuclear issues as such, or even the state of the U.S.–New Zealand bilateral relationship. If future American relations with a prospective Labour party government could not be arranged, the alliance itself could be severely degraded, if not by formal declaration then by attrition. In both New Zealand and Australia, "ANZUS" as a code word for an established and successful security relationship would no longer fit. The U.S.-Australian connection could itself suffer. The defense debate in Australia could well become more polarized between those who would forsake and those who would save the American connection. Any Australian government would in these circumstances find it more difficult to carry out its defense policies confidently. The United States would accordingly become more uneasy about the viability of its facilities and about the value in practice of Australia's professions of commitment. In effect, then, events in New Zealand, alone or eventually in combination with events in Australia, could spell conditions in which ANZUS might become flaccid, or smaller, or even cease to exist.[23]

The odds are against such a scenario in the near future. To lengthen the odds, the United States may need to pause and consider the trade-off between salvaging ANZUS and extending certain concessions or at least practicing considerable composure and circumspection. As seen earlier, the United States has increasingly been seeking calm dialogue with New Zealand Labour Party politicians and other sectors of the public. This, of course, is a cost-free approach. The New Zealand Labour party had indicated that if the United States should try to bring an NPV into the country prior to the general election scheduled for late 1981, it would be interpreted as an unwarranted interference in New Zealand's domestic politics. Since the United States in any event seldom brings such vessels into New Zealand, honoring such an injunction offered little if any inconvenience and reflected simple political prudence. Should the United States need to deal with a Labour Party government in the near future, it probably can do so. For the Labour Party, the NPV issue is not as dramatic as is the issue of nuclear-armed craft. If as presently, under peacetime conditions, ship visits remain occasional, the Labour Party could probably express itself satisfied that NPVs represent no human or other hazards. In regard to armaments, it is conceivable, though by no means certain, that a formula with which both sides could live could be devised. The U.S.-Australian agreement on B-52 stagings might serve as a point of departure for fashioning such an understanding.

The ANZUS Security Relationship in a Global Contest

In the meantime, the United States continues to realize substantial, security-related benefits from its association with New Zealand and Australia. These benefits fall well beyond access to New Zealand and Australian territory or facilities.

Australia's military capabilities are considerably greater than New Zealand's and are rising. Australian forces stand at about 72 thousand and are scheduled to reach 76 thousand by 1985, while New Zealand's forces number 13 thousand. The Australian order of battle includes Leopard tanks, P-3s, F-111s, a submarine flotilla, an aircraft carrier, *Perry* class frigates, and scheduled replacement for its Mirage squadrons with F-18 aircraft. Like Australia, New Zealand flies P-3s and Skyhawks. It has three frigates usable for combat operations and will be acquiring new armored fighting vehicles. Although Australia's defense spending as a proportion of the gross domestic product is scheduled to rise to 3 percent by 1985, there are no long-term plans to increase New Zealand's defense expenditures, which are currently well below 2 percent of GDP and in terms of dollars about one-tenth of Australia's outlays. At bottom, as Prime Minister Muldoon put it, although the United States is entitled to expect a serious New Zealand contribution to the alliance, "I need hardly remind you of the extent that this is, short of unacceptable measures in the social sectors, dependent on increased economic strength."[24]

As we have seen, however, the United States does not and realistically probably should not underestimate the constraints that impinge on New Zealand's defense effort. Indeed, by regional standards, New Zealand as well as Australia have exceptionally well-trained and equipped forces, for the moment discounting questions broached in both nations of whether a core force best suits their defense requirements. The United States derives numerous advantages for its own, regional defense capabilities and objectives through cooperation with Australian and New Zealand forces. Other regional states lack either the sophisticated forces or the political will to engage in the kinds of exercises that are an ongoing feature of ANZUS cooperation. U.S. Marines based in Okinawa who exercise in New Zealand have few if any comparable, open-land terrain opportunities in the region. The special advantages offered for combined service and joint U.S.–Australian–New Zealand operations under the Kangaroo exercise series in Queensland again could not be replicated elsewhere. Plans have been set for both the peacetime patrolling and wartime division of defense responsibilities in the waters adjacent to Australia and New Zealand. Remember that Australia and New Zealand essentially visualize their security as deriving from developments outside their immediate strategic environments. In principle, therefore, New Zealand and Australian military support for the United States under various crisis scenarios in the Asian Pacific basin should not be discounted. Alliance-wide defense activity is itself an asset in legitimizing and collectivizing American security efforts and will continue to have that effect.

Operational and planning aspects of ANZUS military cooperation have by now reached into the Indian Ocean. Australian P-3s have for some years been assisting U.S. surveillance and antisubmarine warfare efforts in the region, including their use of facilities at Diego Garcia, and ANZUS exercises in the Indian Ocean are periodically carried out. Following the outbreak of hostilities between Iraq and Iran in 1980, Australia and New Zealand entered into consultations with the United States regarding possible naval contributions to a multilateral force to protect the Persian Gulf. Although no such force has needed to be formed and no commitments have been extended, contingency planning has proceeded, and both Canberra and Wellington have, in principle, indicated their willingness to consider combat vessel contributions if they feel circumstances warrant them.

It is in the context of Indian Ocean security that we can profitably underline our early point that when Australia and New Zealand have demurred on American requests or preferences, such losses to the United States have not been serious and usually have been more than offset by what Australia and New Zealand do or could contribute.

An instructive example of this came up in October 1980, when after some months of technical preparation, Australia withdrew from participation in the scheduled, Arabian Sea Beacon Compass naval and air exercises with American and British forces. In part, Australia was uneasy about undermining its position among nations outside the Persian Gulf. It wished to avoid offense to African countries, with whom it had established excellent rapport, in part through its constructive role in the Zimbabwe-Rhodesia settlement. Australia has been able to trade on its sound reputation in Africa among the nonwhite, developing countries of the South Pacific community. Australia also wished to be able to insulate its plans to enlarge defense cooperation with Malaysia and Singapore from criticism by some skeptical, Indo-Pacific nations. More pointedly, particularly in the wake of hostilities between Iraq and Iran, Australia wished to forestall damage to itself from appearing too blustering and tied to a dominantly American display of regional force. Australia still had an operating embassy in Iran, was concerned about the safety of its personnel, and could not be sure that just prior to the American elections, the Carter administration would not launch a dramatic, last-moment action to free the hostages. Australia also did not wish to jeopardize its rapidly expanding trade with Persian Gulf and Middle Eastern states. Because of Australia's favorable standing there, the Saudis were considering Australian assistance in developing their national guard and military hospitals.

As it was, even without Australia and with only some adjustments, Beacon Compass was able to go forward. After Beacon Compass was held, partially to demonstrate Australia's ongoing interest in the region's security, an Australian guided missile destroyer undertook a wide-ranging deployment in the Indian Ocean. The decision to withdraw from Beacon Compass was taken on the eve of an Australian national election that, according to the portents, could well have been won by the Labor Party opposition. One apparent, secondary motive to withdrawal from the exercise was that if participation had not been canceled by the incumbent government, a succeeding Labor Party government, less enthusiastic about this type of venture, might have tried to stop it, or at least would likely have had untoward and critical reactions to it. This would have prejudiced U.S.-Australian relations from the start of the new government's tenure. The strain on relations with America was anticipated to be even more severe if Ronald Reagan were elected the following month in the United States.

There are some parallels with Washington's request to Australia earlier in 1980 to consider a contribution to the rapid deployment force. The idea was quickly put down by Australia, as it almost surely would have been even if the United States had not mishandled its approach. Participation in the rapid deployment force would have been politically difficult to uphold in Australia, especially because of the concept's connotation of a ground troop commitment to a distant theater of operations under combat. It could have been resented among some Asian and Indian Ocean littoral states that Australia wished to cultivate politically and commercially. Australia would have made only a marginal contribution to such a collaboration with the United States, while sticking out as the only non-American participant. Australian defense at large, it was announced, would remain a basically independent, national effort.[25]

The preceding illustrations point up that while America's ANZUS partners have at times said no, or only maybe, these responses have not undermined U.S. security interests. In some broader respects, U.S. interests have arguably been advanced. Noncompliance by Australia and New Zealand has enabled them, in some instances, to protect their overseas political and commercial advantages, which in themselves add to Australia's and New Zealand's value within the alliance framework. In other instances, potentially deleterious intra-alliance effects have been averted because sharp domestic debate within the two countries has been contained. Although a case-by-case approach will be necessary, in the future the United States will need to keep in mind that pressing its point when Australia or New Zealand seems out of step could be distinctly counterproductive, not simply because of the danger of upsetting domestic opinion there.

The Contribution of ANZUS to Asia's Security

We now turn to how, through a combination of policy instruments and essentially working independently of the United States, Australia and New Zealand can help to shape regional developments in ways that advance America's regional security objectives. The forecast is that the value of such initiatives to the United States will, if anything, become both more extensive and important. The at-large explanation for this is traceable to the fact that, for reasons of tradition, location, and their reputations and capabilities, New Zealand and Australia enjoy better access and therefore can accomplish more in pursuit of common objectives, than the United States can. These objectives include the stability, defense preparedness, and regional cohesion contributions of various Asian Pacific states. These objectives also entail various forms of a Western security presence, expressed in both concrete and symbolic terms. The inventory of such forms of contributions by Australia and New Zealand is already impressive. It includes Australia's intermittent interlocutory role between China and ASEAN nations, its technical and scientific transfer program in support of China's modernization efforts, and the availability of its enormously abundant natural resources to regional neighbors, notably Japan.

The triangular, U.S.-Japanese-Australian relationship has several merits. It has strategic as well as economic features and promotes broadly regional interests as well as those of the three nations. Hence, American investment capital in Australia (the single largest location of American investment in the East) stimulates the exploitation of natural resources. Australian coal and iron, and prospectively liquefied natural gas and shale, help drive the Japanese economy. The health of that economy brings significant foreign exchange earnings to Australia, is the basis of massive U.S.-Japanese trade, and enables Japan to assist the economies of noncommunist Southeast Asia, to whose viability the United States and its ANZUS partners are deeply committed. For emphasis, however, we especially draw on illustrations from the South Pacific and from Southeast Asia.

In part because it is a relative newcomer to greater South Pacific concerns, in part because it is a superpower known to be engaged in global competition, the United States cannot afford to project a high profile in pan-regional affairs. Australia and New Zealand are, on the other hand, known, trusted, resident, and unintimidating middle-sized powers, already members of a network of regional activities and agencies, including the South Pacific Forum, which excludes the United States. Their regional diplomatic representation is extensive. Their civil aid programs are by far more generous than America's, if U.S. assistance to the Micronesian entities is excluded from the equation. Numerous, regional political elites have been educated in Australia or New Zealand. Even if security-related considerations are discounted, the region is an ANZUS-Commonwealth group, with Australia and New Zealand the dominant actors from within the ANZUS alliance group. Many American analysts feel that New Zealand's political intelligence in the South Pacific is unequaled.

Australia and New Zealand on occasions interpret American policies for the region and at times defend or try to conciliate them. Where security issues are involved, the two ANZUS partners can, for instance, claim a measure of credit for deflecting Soviet regional penetration and thereby for safeguarding their own, and American, security interests. Mostly through Australian and New Zealand influence, Tonga and Western Samoa and later the Cook Islands were dissuaded from granting fishery rights to the Soviets in exchange for dock and airport construction and other developmental assistance. Although regional governments have had their own reasons for resisting, the ANZUS powers have lobbied South Pacific nations not to allow resident Soviet missions, with success being especially apparent in Papua New Guinea.

In 1976, shortly after returning to office, the non-Labor governments in Australia and New Zealand were instrumental in setting aside an earlier South Pacific Forum declaration that had endorsed a regional nuclear-free zone, which in time could have inconvenienced American strategic mobility or embarrassed U.S. relations with resident countries. Australia and the New Zealand National Party government have continued to dampen regional notions of such a zone. Their credibility has been enhanced by their vigorous condemnation of French nuclear testing in Polynesia. Ironically, their regional credentials have been improved because they have joined the South Pacific community's criticism of U.S. plans to store spent nuclear fuel from Asian nations temporarily on an American-held Pacific island, even though the American proposal is designed to serve the cause of nonproliferation.

Australian and New Zealand defense cooperation and assistance programs also contribute to overall regional security objectives. Most of the region's nations are too small to require formal military establishments. But their police, coastal surveillance, and national developmental tasks require equipment and professional help that, at small cost but high political value for the West, are provided pre-eminently by Australia and New Zealand. The armed forces of Papua New Guinea, Fiji, and Tonga, the only forces in the region, are almost exclusively trained and supplied by Australia and New Zealand. Some Australian troops are still on loan to or serve as formed units in support roles for Papua New Guinea, the largest South Pacific country by far and the link between the region and Southeast Asia; it requires forces for internal security as well as border tasks. Fijian troops, logistically backed by Australia and New Zealand, have performed in international supervisory and peacekeeping roles. In 1980, the passage of the New Hebrides to independent status as Vanuatu was being compromised by an internal revolt. The troops of Papua New Guinea that were invited to restore order were airlifted in by Australia, which also provided spotter aircraft and logistical, communication, and other rear echelon support for the operation. Within the Pacific community Australia was commended for this role, as well as for having had the foresight and skill to mold a professional, defense force for Papua New Guinea. Afterward, Vanuatu asked Australia to help it develop its own internal security establishment. More broadly, together with New Zealand and the United States, Australia construed a supportive role in Vanuatu as a significant, precautionary exercise. Anglo-French and other local stresses, Prime Minister Malcolm Fraser explained, raised "the possibility that the example of Vanuatu might affect the situation in other island countries of the region. And there would be the possibility of outside interference to exploit the situation."[26]

Australia and New Zealand have done much for common, ANZUS alliance security in the South Pacific region. Indeed, a leading American authority on the region has cautioned that, however indispensable the Australian and New Zealand role, the United States should not allow its own, albeit secondary, position to be entirely overshadowed.[27]

Australia's and New Zealand's security value to the United States in the Southeast Asian region is especially prominent. In general, the promotional efforts of Canberra and Wellington on behalf of ASEAN as a collectivity complement present American objectives of regional visibility and insulation not only from an assertive Vietnam but also from Soviet and Chinese insinuations. Both Australia and New Zealand are extensively involved in training members of ASEAN national defense forces. During 1979 and 1980, New Zealand trained about 260 and Australia, 580 overseas military personnel, and Australia then planned to increase its intake to 1,200. In both countries, the majority of trainees and staff and command school guests are from Southeast Asia. New Zealand and especially Australian exercises with Southeast Asian defense forces are by now commonplace. Through their continuing adhesion to the Manila Pact, Australia and New Zealand will continue to provide a wider umbrella for American efforts to emphasize the integrity of Thailand, Southeast Asia's front-line state, a cause broadly upheld by Thailand's ASEAN partners.

Australia in particular has taken a keen interest in maintaining close and supportive relations with Indonesia. Indonesia is ASEAN's largest and most influential member. It is a major oil producer and a member of OPEC; it is also well endowed with other natural resources. It dominates the maritime passageways between the Pacific and Indian Oceans and is the Southeast Asian link, via Papua New Guinea, to the South Pacific region. The Suharto regime in Indonesia has, moreover, been politically stable.

Among other things, Australia has assisted in the negotiation of provisions for unencumbered U.S. naval transit through the Indonesian straits, has helped to train and equip Indonesian forces, and helped to defuse a potentially disruptive regional dispute on the Irian Jaya–Papua New Guinea border. By late 1976, Australia assumed a generally permissive view of Indonesia's incorporation of East Timor. Under both the Ford and Carter administrations, the United States found some plausibility in the Indonesian argument that without a takeover of East Timor an unstable or radical regime could have emerged and separatist sentiment elsewhere in Indonesia might have been fueled. The United States also, at large, was reluctant and will continue to be reluctant to alienate Indonesia.

Australia's and New Zealand's most direct Southeast Asian security contributions lie in Malaysia and Singapore. The Five Power Defense Agreement (FPDA) linking Australia, New Zealand, and Britain to Malaysia and Singapore continues, even though regional command by New Zealand, Australia, and Britain ended by the mid-1970s. In the event of an actual or threatened external attack on Malaysia or Singapore, the signatories promise "immediate" consultations on what measures to take. The FPDA carries no less weight and obligation, and may well have more credibility, than the formal Manila Pact that associates the ANZUS powers with the security of Thailand and nominally the Philippines. Moreover, there is a tangible Australian and New Zealand presence in Singapore and Malaysia. A New Zealand infantry battalion with support units continues to be garrisoned in Singapore. The Royal Australian Navy deploys a destroyer in Southeast Asian waters for most of the year, and a submarine for somewhat less time, both of which are based in Singapore. The Integrated Air Defense System, headquartered at Butterworth, on the western coast of west Malaysia, includes personnel from all FPDA parties. Two squadrons of Australian Mirage fighters have long been based there, two P-3s have just been based there, and an infantry company is deployed there regularly. A half dozen of the Mirages are detached from Butterworth to the Singapore airbase at Tengah, in training and for integrated defense roles.

This presence has and will continue to serve regional American security interests. Australian and New Zealand forces, at times augmented from home, measurably contribute to Malaysian and Singapore defense capabilities through training and joint exercises. In particular, because of their acceptability, Australia and New Zealand have significantly enhanced Malaysian-Singapore defense coordination and confidence, in the context of delicate ethnic-political relations between these countries. Second, undertakings such as the New Zealand Battalion and the Integrated Air Defense System have been construed as an informal ANZUS presence in Southeast Asia. The presence has not been too overt and is essentially minus the United States, but it is still valuable, at minimum as a symbolic expression of Western regional interests and of visibly amicable, resident nation and ANZUS power cooperation. These assets are likely to be underscored and reinforced by ambitious air, sea, and (in Australia) land exercises held among the five powers in 1981, and foreseeably continuing in later years. No such exercises had been conducted for a decade; the initiative was Australian, but with full American concurrence and appreciation. It would not be accurate to describe this as an Australian or ANZUS effort to build toward a new, compact, subregional, though informal, alliance system. It is, however, regarded in ANZUS quarters as a contribution to subregional security awareness and defense preparedness and more generally as a manifestation of resolve in the context of a communist and Soviet-associated Indochina. Although the New Zealand Battalion and the Australian Mirages are scheduled to return home in the next few years, the FPDA will remain intact, and other features of Australia's and New Zealand's presence and cooperation such as ships, training programs, and P-3s will continue.

Australian and New Zealand defense contributions in Malaysia and Singapore have also taken the form of tangible facilitation and augmentation of American naval and air capabilities. Two such contributions are particularly instructive, in part because they illustrate interregional security linkages between Southeast Asia and the Indian Ocean. For some time, Australians stationed at Tengah provided unpublicized, but politically mutually acceptable, service for American reconnaissance and transport air traffic transiting through Singapore between the Pacific and Indian Oceans. The arrangement was disclosed and formalized in 1978, when it was no longer necessary for Singapore to conceal the operation and as its own perceptions of regional security sharpened. Indeed, workable defense arrangements such as this, and with New Zealand in some analogous respects, facilitated Singapore's invitation to the United States to consider Singapore as a new basing site after Indian Ocean security became a high priority in Washington. Australian P-3s have for some time been refueling at Butterworth. Base deployment of two of the aircraft will enhance ANZUS-Western regional surveillance capabilities in the South China Sea, including of Soviet naval and air movements in and out of Vietnam, over the Strait of Malacca joining the Pacific and Indian Oceans, and over the Indian Ocean itself. At present, the United States enjoys no basing rights between the Philippines and Diego Garcia.

Conclusion

Undiminished Soviet-American competition and insinuating efforts of the Soviets, the complexity and difficult management of evolving national and subregional politics, and the various factors that constrain American influence are foreseen in Asia and the Pacific. Australia and New Zealand offer an imposing and, in some respects, irreplaceable array of assets that serve to promote American security interests within the Asian Pacific basin and into the Indian Ocean. It is therefore of first importance that the United States foster its links and standing with New Zealand and Australia. In doing so, the United States cannot overlook that its ANZUS alliance partners are not unconstrained in what they can and are prepared to do and that some strains and disappointments are inevitable. It must, in its own interest, exercise care and composure in dealing with them. In comparison with the dividends that the United States can reasonably expect to draw from such handling, the costs are indeed affordable.

Notes

1. See Larry Lescaze, *Washington Post,* June 2, 1979. For Selden's remarks, see *Age* (Melbourne), April 18, 1978.

2. Marshall Green, interview with Ken Randall in *National Times,* February 1, 1975.

3. See "Australian Attitudes Toward Security and Economic Relations with the United States," *Morgan Gallup Poll* conducted in April 1978 for the U.S. International Communication Agency, Office of Research and Evaluation, published October 19, 1978. Also see the USICA-sponsored poll, taken April 1980 and published in USICA, *Research Memorandum,* May 27, 1980.

4. See *Morgan Gallup Poll,* no. 672, November–December 1979.

5. "Age Poll," published in *Age,* May 12, 1980.

6. *Morgan Gallup Poll,* no. 713, April 1980, and no. 788A, January 1981. On American facilities, see *Saulwick and Associates Poll,* published in *Sydney Morning Herald,* June 29, 1981.

7. Arthur W. Hummel, Jr., *Hearings on U.S. Policies in Southeast Asia,* Special Subcommittee on Investigations, Committee on International Relations, House of Representatives, 94th Congress, 2d session, September 28, 1976, p. 25.

8. Richard Holbrooke, cited by Michael Richardson in *Australian Financial Review,* January 19, 1978. Holbrooke was assistant secretary of state for east Asia and the Pacific during the Carter administration.

9. ANZUS council communiqué (Wellington), July 28, 1977.

10. See John Hamilton in *Herald* (Melbourne), June 9, 1978, and Mike Steketee in *Sydney Morning Herald,* June 10, 1978. Andrew Peacock disclosed the letter's contents during a June 1978 press conference following ANZUS council meetings in Washington.

11. Lester Wolff, remarks cited in *Prospects for Regional Stability: Asia and the Pacific,* report submitted by a special study mission to Asia and the Pacific, January 2–22, 1978, under the auspices of the Subcommittee on Asian and Pacific Affairs, Committee on International Relations, House of Representatives, 95th Congress, 2d session, 1978, p. 18.

12. Holbrooke, testimony of July 31, 1978, *Emerging Pacific Island Community,* hearing before the Subcommittee on East Asian and Pacific Affairs, Committee on Foreign Relations, Senate, 95th Congress, 2d session, p. 9.

13. Alexander Haig, reply to question from Senator Charles Percy, *Nomination of Alexander M. Haig, Jr.,* hearing before the Committee on Foreign Relations, Senate, 97th Congress, 1st session, part 2, January 14, 1981, p. 24.

14. See, for instance, remarks by Hayden and others at the ALP federal conference, Adelaide, cited in *Canberra Times,* July 20, 1979; by Hayden following his tour of the interior facilities, cited by Russell Skelton in *Age,* March 19, 1981; and his views on North-West Cape summarized by Marian Wilkinson in *National Times,* May 10, 1981.

15. Hayden and Killen, "AM" radio broadcast interview of May 15, 1978, transcript. Also see Killen's remarks in Defence *Press Release,* no. 70/78, May 16, 1978.

16. Killen, *Commonwealth Parliamentary Debates,* House of Representatives, May 25, 1978, pp. 2457-459.

17. See, for instance, Lionel Bowen (deputy ALP House leader), remarks reported in Sydney *Daily Telegraph,* July 12, 1980, and in *Sydney Morning Herald,* September 22, 1980; Hayden reported in *Sydney Morning Herald,* August 25, 1980; and the various parliamentary exchanges on the subject in *Commonwealth Parliamentary Debates,* House of Representatives, March 12, 1981, *passim.* For the Australian Council of Trade Unions resolution opposing nuclear weapons in Australia, see *Australian Financial Review,* November 21, 1980.

18. For the agreement, see Fraser, *Commonwealth Parliamentary Debates,* House of Representatives, March 11, 1981, pp. 666-67. For earlier expositions by Fraser, see his remarks in Darwin of September 19, 1980, cited by Michelle Grattan, *Age,* September 20, 1980; and amplification by Peter Robinson, *Australian Financial Review,* December 11, 1980. For American interpretation of the agreement, see U.S. Embassy, Canberra, *Press Release* of March 30, 1981, "U.S.-Australian Agreement on Transit of Darwin by USAF B-52 aircraft on Training and Sea Surveillance Missions."

19. W. E. Rowling, interview with Richard Long in *Dominion* (Wellington), June 4, 1980.

20. For example, see the statement of the U.S. Embassy in Wellington, reproduced in *Star* (Christchurch), May 21, 1979; remarks by Ann Martindell, U.S. ambassador to New Zealand, reported in *Press* (Christchurch), September 11, 1979; comments of Evelyn Colbert, recently retired U.S. deputy assistant secretary of state for East Asian and Pacific Affairs, in *Dominion,* September 30, 1980, and *Press,* October 3, 1980.

21. *Press,* May 16, 1980.

22. Rowling, cited in *Dominion,* May 17, 1980, and his *Press Release* of June 10, 1980. For earlier expositions by Rowling, see interviews with John Henderson, *New Zealand International Review,* September/October 1977, and with Derek Round, ibid., September/October 1978.

23. For defenses of ANZUS, especially in the light of Labour Party criticisms, see

Muldoon, address to the Otago/Southland meeting of the National Party of May 16, 1980, transcript; Brian Talboys, address in Wellington of June 9, 1980, transcript, and his *Press Statement* of June 11, 1980; remarks by James Webster, Australian high commissioner to New Zealand, cited in *Evening Post* (Wellington), June 10, 1980; Evelyn Colbert, transcript of remarks reproduced in *New Zealand International Review,* November/December 1980. For a helpful collection of various dimensions of New Zealand defense policy, with special reference to the alliance, see *New Zealand and ANZUS—A Defence Policy for the 80's* (Wellington: Ministry of Foreign Affairs, 1980), Special Bulletin 1980/2.

24. Muldoon, address of March 18, 1977, National Press Club, Canberra, cited in *New Zealand Foreign Affairs Review* 27 (January–March 1977): 23–24.

25. See, for instance, J. R. MacKellar (acting foreign minister), statement of March 2, 1980, in *Age,* March 3, 1980; and Fraser, interview with John Edwards, *Bulletin,* September 9, 1980. For partial accounts of the original request, see Brian Toohey, *Australian Financial Review,* February 29, 1980; and John Edwards, *Bulletin,* March 18, 1980.

26. Fraser, address to the Tasmanian State (Liberal Party) Council, August 15, 1980, cited in *Commonwealth Record* 5, no. 32: 1209.

27. John C. Dorrance, "Oceania and the United States: An Analysis of U.S. Interests and Policy in the South Pacific," Research Directorate, National Defense University, *National Security Affairs Monograph* no. 80-82 (February 1980): 35–36.

7 | THE U.S. ROLE IN EAST AND SOUTHEAST ASIA

Franklin B. Weinstein

The past decade has been a time of extraordinary uncertainty on both sides of the Pacific about the future role of the United States in east and Southeast Asia. The defeat of U.S.-backed forces in Vietnam and the forging of a new relationship with the People's Republic of China are only the most dramatic of a series of developments that have called into question basic assumptions underlying American thinking about Asian security for most of the period since World War II.

The Need for a New Conceptual Framework

The Changing Strategic Context and Rising Uncertainty About America's Role in Asia

The security structure established in the 1940s and 1950s assumed the existence of a monolithic communist threat, with Moscow at the helm.[1] Until the 1970s, the Soviet Union possessed little capability to project its forces directly in east and Southeast Asia, and Soviet power in the region was manifested largely via proxies. In the event of hostilities involving American forces, U.S. naval and air supremacy could be taken for granted. The basic principle underlying the responses by noncommunist nations to security threats was reliance on a set of alliances committing the United States to the defense of allied states against communist expansionism. The establishment of a network of U.S. bases, the spreading of a U.S. nuclear umbrella over much of the region, the deployment of U.S. ground forces to lend credibility to U.S. commitments, and the extension of military aid to allies and potential allies were essential elements of this security system. The military relationships were reinforced by a set of economic and political links with noncommunist states, predicated on the assumption of complementary economic interests. The highest value was attached to enhancing and maintaining the solidarity of the noncommunist alliances. The capability of the United States to lead this coalition was little disputed.

By the late 1970s, bitter conflict among the communist powers—between the Soviet Union and China, China and Vietnam, and Vietnam and Kampuchea (Cambodia)—had become one of the central facts of Asian international relations. The principal military conflicts—existing and threatened—pitted communist against communist. Détente between the United States and the Soviet Union, which had begun to flower in the 1960s and had seemed in the early 1970s to promise a new era of superpower cooperation, had crumbled by the end of the decade; U.S. disillusionment with détente, evident since the mid-1970s, crystallized after the Soviet invasion of Afghanistan. Meanwhile, the Soviet Union had strengthened its ground and air forces deployed in the Soviet Far East and developed a formidable naval presence in the region; in 1979, the Soviets began making use of military base facilities at Cam Ranh Bay and Da Nang. It could no longer be safely assumed that U.S. naval and air forces would be able to operate in a future east Asian contingency without Soviet challenge. Many analysts asserted that confidence in the ability of the United States to project its military power in Asia effectively had been eroded not only by the Vietnam fiasco but also by the inability of the Americans to act decisively in Iran, Afghanistan, and elsewhere.

America's allies seemed increasingly inclined to question the credibility of U.S. security commitments and the stability of U.S. leadership, as the United States during the 1970s lurched from a preoccupation with Vietnam to post-Vietnam War policies that implied continued retrenchment and then moved to a forward defense policy focused on the creation of a rapid deployment force and the strengthening of U.S. allies in Asia. U.S. forces withdrew from Thailand in the mid-1970s, but by 1979 the U.S. commitment to Thailand had been reaffirmed and military aid dramatically increased. Plans to withdraw U.S. ground combat forces from South Korea were announced in 1977 and suspended in 1979; the Reagan administration has indicated that it may augment the U.S. air presence in South Korea. U.S. bases in Thailand were closed, and the future of America's Philippine bases was cast into doubt by Manila's demands for renegotiation of the terms under which access to the bases could be preserved; an agreement was reached in January 1979 that ensured American access to the Philippine bases until 1984, but rising opposition to President Ferdinand Marcos's leadership raises doubt about the future of the agreement.

Diplomatic and economic policies emanating from Washington have added to the sense of uncertainty about the future role of the United States in Asia. Because they have often been ambiguously defined and inconsistently implemented, American foreign policies have generated considerable confusion both in the United States and abroad. The following examples illustrate this confusion:

1. U.S. intentions concerning the normalization of relations with Vietnam have been difficult to fathom. In 1977 and 1978, the United States appeared to show an intermittent interest in normalization, but negotiations with Hanoi were sidetracked in 1978 by Washington's apparent desire to avoid impeding progress toward the normalization and further development of U.S.-China relations. Since Vietnam's intervention in Kampuchea, the United States has seemingly abandoned any effort to establish a relationship with Vietnam.

2. Washington's policy on human rights, consisting of sporadic expressions of concern about conditions in several Asian countries unaccompanied by action, has puzzled and frustrated partisans on both sides of the issue. Even though President Reagan's nomination of a critic of human rights initiatives as the principal Department of State official responsible for human rights affairs was rebuffed, there is little doubt that the administration intends a complete reversal of its predecessor's policy on human rights.

3. Policies to deal with energy problems have been ineffective, and Washington's initially vigorous efforts to prevent nuclear weapons proliferation as an outgrowth of nuclear energy development have been carried out inconsistently. The United States reversed its policy opposing the sale of nuclear fuel to India despite India's refusal to accept comprehensive safeguards and to give assurances that it would refrain from future nuclear detonations. After having urged Japan to develop reprocessing facilities, Washington opposed such facilities in the name of nonproliferation and finally muted its opposition when the Japanese proved unyielding. Even if these reversals were justified, the overall impression was one of a lack of direction. The Reagan administration, which stunned the Japanese when it dropped a proposed program for international development of synthetic fuels, is likely to effect a complete reversal of its predecessor's original nonproliferation policy. For governments that must make long-term plans, which are essential in the energy field, such reversals are disconcerting at best.

4. The Japanese have been puzzled by conflicting signals from the United States on the degree of importance attached to Japan's assuming an expanded defense burden. Although Washington and Tokyo have

established closer cooperation in defense planning, the relationship has been rocked by a series of economic conflicts that ultimately could undermine the perception of shared interests on which the security alliance depends. The Reagan administration has pushed hard for an expansion of Japan's military role, and Tokyo has appeared to be responsive, but it was evident from statements following the May 1981 summit meeting and the June consultations on defense in Hawaii and Washington that there is a substantial gap between the two sides.

5. By the end of the 1970s, there was a growing realization that the weakness of the U.S. economy, the lack of an effective energy policy, and the declining productivity of U.S. industry were deep-rooted problems that not only could affect adversely the economies of other countries but also could seriously diminish the capacity of the United States to exercise effective international leadership.

The failure to make clear the conceptual framework within which the Asian policies of the United States are cast has made it difficult to understand policy changes and has contributed significantly to the uncertainty surrounding the future U.S. role in east and Southeast Asia. The adjustment of policies to fit the post–Vietnam War strategic context has been unsure and piecemeal, with policies seemingly patched together in response to domestic political concerns, pressures from allies, and presidential predispositions. There has been no clear statement of the goals and instruments of a security policy attuned to the realities of a new era. This deficiency has been most glaringly apparent with regard to two major departures of U.S. Asian policy in recent years: (1) the Carter administration's aborted decision to withdraw ground combat forces from Korea and (2) the development of a quasi-alliance relationship with China. The Korea policy was presented in a manner that confused both U.S. allies and the Congress; some members of Congress who were basically sympathetic to the withdrawal asserted that the long-term goals and assumptions underlying the move were never made clear. Similarly, both the Japanese and Europeans have expressed concern that the United States is now drifting into a military relationship with China without having thought through the potential implications of such ties. Their fears were reinforced by Secretary of State Alexander Haig's surprise announcement during his June 1981 visit to Beijing that Washington was prepared, in principle, to sell arms to China.

The Japanese, and other U.S. allies, frequently ask for a clarification of Washington's overall strategic plan. They are increasingly inclined to view the United States as a nation prone to dramatic emotional swings from one extreme to the other; the hyperbolic rhetoric accompanying Washington's reaction to the Soviet invasion of Afghanistan is cited as a case in point.

Without some clear guidelines concerning the basic assumptions, overall goals, and expectations of U.S. Asian policies, it is difficult to assess the implications of U.S. policy initiatives—to understand, for example, why a withdrawal of U.S. troops from Korea may not imply a diminution of commitments in the region or what criteria would be used to define the limits of a U.S. relationship with China. Without such guidelines, it is hard to build a political consensus in support of such policies, either with allies or domestically.

The lack of direction that has characterized U.S. Asian policies over the past decade runs far deeper than the failings of any particular administration or set of leaders. There is a fundamental need for a new conceptual framework that reflects the requirements of the strategic context of the 1980s. It is necessary to clarify the assumptions being made by the United States and the other major actors in east Asia concerning interests and threats. Then, consistent with those assumptions, it will be appropriate to spell out the basic principles governing U.S. efforts to maximize security and respond to perceived threats.

Perceived Threats to Security

There is considerable overlap in the way the United States, Japan, China, and the Soviet Union view their security concerns. Two central organizing themes structure current thinking about security. First, the United States, Japan, and China are preoccupied with the problem of how to deal with the Soviet Union, especially the rising challenge of Soviet military power. Potential Vietnamese expansionism is seen not only as dangerous in itself but also as a possible projection of Soviet power, and, at least for the Americans and the Japanese, the same may be said of North Korean expansionism. For the Soviet Union, the fear of encirclement by a U.S.-Chinese-Japanese entente is a major concern.

Second, all four nations feel a profound sense of vulnerability with regard to their economies. They all face serious difficulties in ensuring a continued supply of energy at reasonable cost. This concern is most intense in Japan, completely dependent on imports, but it is a major preoccupation as well for the Soviets, who may face an energy shortage in the mid-1980s (earlier CIA predictions of such shortages were modified in mid-1981), and for the Chinese, who lack the capital and technology required to exploit their own extensive reserves. The Soviet economy manifests a wide array of weaknesses, which may be difficult to overcome unless the USSR can enlist Japanese and American support in the development of Siberia and in supplying certain critical commodities. For the United States, the central economic concern is declining productivity, which may directly involve

Japan because competition from Japanese goods is a contributing factor in the decline of U.S. industrial output (though it may also be viewed more positively as a challenge that may compel the United States to raise its productivity). China, at a very different stage in its economic development, sees the modernization of its economy as the most pressing national imperative.

The two sets of issues—relations with the Soviet Union and economic vulnerabilities—have some interconnections. In the United States and Japan, there is concern that the growth of Soviet military power, and Moscow's increasing boldness in exercising that power, could lead to an interruption of energy supplies from the Middle East. For China, the need for capital and technology to implement the goals of modernization creates a degree of dependence on the Western industrial democracies; a united front against a common Soviet threat may help to attract the needed aid and, in Chinese eyes, to justify the acceptance of such a dependency relationship. From the standpoint of the Soviets, however, the development of close, multifaceted ties among the other three powers is not only a threat but also diminishes the possibility that the United States or Japan will provide the kinds of economic support that could help invigorate the Soviet economy.

At present, there is an apparent coalescence of views among the United States, Japan, and China—especially with regard to the perceived Soviet threat. The predominant mood in the United States is one of preoccupation with and reaction to Soviet expansionism and the buildup of the USSR's military capabilities. This mood, which became evident during the last year of the Carter administration, has dramatically intensified since the assumption of power by the Reagan administration. One commentator has characterized the current trend as a movement on the part of the U.S. government toward a revived containment policy, with China having switched sides.[2] The United States has not endorsed China's call for an anti-Soviet united front, but U.S. policy appears to be drifting toward an anti-Soviet coalition as Washington intensifies its tilt toward China and presses Japan to undertake a larger defense role. The Reagan administration, seeking to deter Soviet intervention in Poland, threatened to establish a closer relationship with China, including military assistance. Subsequently, Secretary of State Haig offered such assistance in principle, even though the Soviets had shown restraint in Poland. How firmly rooted this trend toward closer relations with China may be is not clear, especially in light of the Reagan administration's strong feelings concerning Taiwan. But it is quite understandable that the embryonic military aid relationship that appeared to be developing during the Carter administration's final year has apparently excited even greater interest on the part of an administration that attaches the highest priority to the mobilization of forces against the expansion of Soviet power.

Current U.S. attitudes—and especially the emotionalism attached to these attitudes—reflect the profound sense of disillusionment with détente. Feelings of betrayal by the Soviet Union may be attributed, at least in part, to the overselling of détente. The question that must be answered is whether the exaggerated promise of détente—merely the latest in a series of oversold U.S. foreign policies—represents a phenomenon that is endemic to the U.S. system. Is it possible to build public support for a policy without exaggerating its prospective benefits?

In Japan, one can discern a similar conservative trend. The Japanese clearly share the U.S. concern about the Soviet buildup but less deeply. The Japanese government has publicly identified the Soviet Union as a threat to security, and Tokyo has gradually moved toward acceptance of a limited expansion of its defense role. But growing Japanese awareness of the Soviet threat has been accompanied by the frequent expression of Japanese reservations about a confrontational policy toward the Soviet Union. Some Japanese leaders have stressed that steps taken by Tokyo in response to the Soviet invasion of Afghanistan should be understood as part of an effort to demonstrate solidarity with and loyalty to the United States, not as an indication of heightened concern about any Soviet threat to Japan. The Japanese emphasize the continued importance of détente and the restoration of cooperative relations with the USSR. Many influential Japanese believe that the United States' reaction to the Soviet invasion of Afghanistan was excessively emotional and out of proportion to the threat posed by Moscow's action in that country. They believe it is a mistake to conclude that the Soviet action requires dismantling the entire structure of détente. On the contrary, they argue the need for a redefined policy of détente, based on a clearer understanding of the policy's limits and rules for its effective management. Japanese of this viewpoint are troubled by the apparent move toward a de facto U.S.-Japanese-Chinese alliance in part because it seems likely to freeze the Soviets in a belligerent stance.

The predominant view among the Japanese appears to be that security must be considered in broader terms—hence their concept of "comprehensive security," embracing a variety of nonmilitary concerns. Most would agree that the potential loss of energy resources constitutes a more pressing danger than any Soviet military challenge, although, as noted earlier, the two challenges may be linked. On the other hand, the Soviet Union, like China, is seen as a potential source of energy, not merely as a threat to Japan's energy supplies.

The basic elements of Chinese policy are cooperation with the advanced industrial democracies in order to promote China's four modernizations and the development of a united front to meet the Soviet threat. A recent analysis by two China specialists emphasizes that the domestic dimension is of "decisive importance."[3] Economic modernization is the principal preoccupation of the Chinese. The level of political uncertainty remains high, however, and former adherents of the Cultural Revolution may still be a force about which the leadership needs to be concerned. Even if those political elements were not a source of concern, the leadership's modernization strategy involves certain unavoidable political risks, since the government must deliver on its promises to many constituencies. As expectations rise, the potential for disillusionment—and backlash against the leadership—also rises. If indeed the Chinese leaders (1) attach the highest priority to modernization, (2) believe that modernization requires Western assistance, and (3) are concerned about the political risks inherent in their modernization strategy, then it may be appropriate to ask whether the Soviet threat is, at least in part, being used by them not only to attract Western aid but also to help ward off potential political criticism. If so, what does this suggest about the likelihood that current Chinese attitudes regarding the Soviet threat will persist?

The United States, Japan, and China thus share a concern about the Soviet threat but with sharply varying degrees of intensity and with different motivations. There may also be different views among the three concerning the likelihood that present trends will persist. Many Japanese, emphasizing their uneasiness at the development of a military relationship between the United States and China, cite the fragility of the political balance in Beijing. They are sharply aware of the possibility that a different Chinese leadership several years hence may use military assets acquired from the United States for purposes that Japan could find troubling. American policymakers do not, in the view of many Japanese, seem sufficiently sensitive to the possibility that Chinese attitudes may change.

The Soviets see themselves as increasingly vulnerable.[4] They are beset by an intensifying fear of encirclement, a concern that their naval and air forces in Asia may be inadequate, and a realization that they will not be able to achieve their economic goals without the cooperation of the United States and Japan. The Soviets have found themselves increasingly isolated, except for their ties to Vietnam. This is not to suggest that the Soviets' fear of encirclement by a U.S.-Japanese-Chinese entente has made them meek and retiring; on the contrary, their sense of vulnerability may lead them to adopt a more belligerent posture and to undertake aggressive actions. The economic pressures bearing on the Soviet Union in the mid-1980s, centered on but not limited to a possible energy shortage, eventually may affect Moscow's attitude toward the United States and Japan, but it is hard to predict how Soviet attitudes might change.

The foregoing analysis suggests a paradox. The United States, Japan, and China are said to be deeply concerned about the expansion of Soviet power and Moscow's increasing boldness; the United States, in contrast, is portrayed as indecisive and lagging militarily. Yet, at the same time, the Soviets are said to feel increasingly vulnerable. Is it not strange that both sides feel increasingly vulnerable simultaneously? This paradox points to the need to consider carefully the contrasting evaluations of the gravity of the Soviet threat. Which view is closer to circumstances that can reliably be predicted for the 1980s—the currently prevailing American view, shared with even greater intensity by the Chinese, or the more sanguine perspective that seems to dominate Japanese thinking?

A Conceptual Framework for the 1980s

A conceptual framework within which policies may be constructed to meet perceived challenges to security depends, in the first instance, on how one answers the question just posed concerning the gravity of the Soviet threat. The previous discussion suggests the existence of two sharply contrasting approaches to security. These approaches lie at the opposite ends of a continuum, and they reflect dramatically different interpretations of threats to security, opportunities for cooperation, and effective ways to respond to each. The two approaches, described in their extreme forms, may be contrasted as follows: (1) overriding Soviet threat requires strengthening of alliances and eventual creation of a united front; (2) diffuse threats and opportunities call for a modus vivendi with the USSR and establishment of a multiple linkage system.

To illustrate these contrasting approaches, we may identify four points along the continuum. One extreme assumes that a single overriding threat—emanating from the Soviet Union—is the source of virtually all security problems and that the most effective way to deal with this threat is through a buildup of military forces opposed to the USSR, strengthening of alliance and alignment relationships, and, ultimately, the development of a united front aimed at convincing Moscow to give up its expansionist designs in the face of overwhelming opposition. Opportunities for cooperation may be recognized, but they are dismissed as undesirable to pursue because they will only strengthen the adversary. A corollary is that there must be unyielding opposition to any proposals for cooperation with Vietnam and North Korea, since such cooperation would have the effect of strengthening, albeit indirectly, the Soviet Union. The Chinese view comes close to this extreme, although Beijing would exempt North Korea from the adversary list.

A less extreme version of that approach singles out the Soviet threat as the central concern among a variety of potential challenges, emphasizes the strengthening of existing U.S. alliance relationships and increased military contributions by allies, and proposes a cautious movement toward military cooperation with China if the Soviets continue to behave in a belligerent manner. Such an approach resembles the one elaborated by Richard Solomon in his introduction to the Rand study, *Asian Security in the 1980s*.[5]

Moving to the other half of the continuum, we may identify a third approach, which coincides in certain respects with the thinking of many Japanese. It focuses on comprehensive security and perceives military and economic challenges from a variety of sources, as well as opportunities for cooperation with both allied and potential adversary-nations. This approach attaches importance to existing alliances but accords a high priority to the search for ways to establish a modus vivendi with the Soviet Union; it seeks the establishment of a degree of equilibrium in relations among powers. Such a modus vivendi would spell out the areas in which U.S. and Soviet interests coincide and would specify issues on which no agreement is possible. The central point is that the Soviet Union needs to be regarded not merely as a threat but also as a major power with which it is possible to cooperate in important areas. By the term *modus vivendi* I mean to signify the possibility of limited cooperation without any connotation of relaxing, as was the case with détente.

An important aspect of this third approach is the emphasis on establishing multiple linkages.[6] The idea of multiple linkages goes beyond a modus vivendi with the Soviets to signify a diversity of crosscutting relationships linking communist and noncommunist nations on different issues. Relationships with Vietnam and North Korea are possible within a multiple linkages regime, even though those countries may continue to be regarded as potential adversaries. The main tenet of the multiple linkages concept is that conflict, when it arises, will be fragmented along numerous lines; the danger of the kind of polarization that can lead to hostilities is reduced.

Finally, at the end of the continuum lies a more extreme form of the multiple linkages approach in which existing alliance structures have been replaced and a genuine equilibrium achieved.

These approaches are not mutually exclusive. For example, one can imagine a fractured united front in which the various members may not pursue identical policies. Military strength, and a degree of cooperation, will be important whichever approach is adopted; similarly, efforts to engage the Soviet Union in certain forms of cooperative activity are unlikely to be abandoned even if the emphasis is on building a united front against the Soviets. A viable framework for U.S. policies in east and Southeast Asia will have to incorporate, in some reasonable balance, elements from both halves of the continuum. The task is to identify compatible elements and to strike the optimum balance. For example, fostering the diversity of crosscutting relationships—which is central to the multiple linkages approach— is likely to be incompatible with an all-encompassing emphasis on alliance solidarity, but certain aspects of an alliance relationship can be made stronger, even if the overall relationship becomes less monolithic. The fundamental question is: Can support be sustained for a complex policy that seeks reconciliation as well as confrontation and includes economic competition among allied states?

In my opinion, a viable framework for U.S. policies in east and Southeast Asia in the 1980s should emphasize the following elements: (1) the relatively diffuse nature of threats to security, as opposed to overwhelming emphasis on the Soviet threat and associated Vietnamese and North Korean challenges; (2) the strengthening of certain aspects of alliance relationships, while encouraging greater independence in a number of areas on the part of allies; and (3) efforts to move toward multiple linkages rather than the conflict-laden polarization inherent in efforts to construct an anti-Soviet united front.

The currently prevailing U.S. view, not to mention the Chinese perspective, exaggerates the seriousness of the Soviet threat in Asia and of the challenges posed by Hanoi and Pyongyang. It is necessary at the outset to distinguish between Soviet capabilities in Asia, where Moscow has certain pronounced weaknesses, and the threat that Soviet forces may pose elsewhere in the world.

There is no question that the Soviets will continue to build up their forces in the Asian region. The reasons for that buildup are complex, including Moscow's image of itself as a global power, bureaucratic pressures within the Kremlin, the need to protect the USSR's strategic forces, and a concern about the possibility of future conflict with China. The Soviets will undoubtedly exploit whatever targets of opportunity emerge in the region, but their military buildup is not necessarily aimed at invading or intimidating Japan or any other noncommunist countries in east or Southeast Asia.

Clearly, the Soviet buildup is a matter of concern, and it is essential that the United States and its allies maintain a balance with Soviet forces. But given the fact that the Soviet Union has traditionally been a land power, the increase in Soviet naval capabilities has been especially dramatic. One cannot expect that Soviet capabilities will expand at a linear rate. Nor can the United States expect to maintain the kind of unchallenged supremacy at sea and in the air that it enjoyed for more than two decades after World

War II. That supremacy has been a comfortable situation for the United States and its allies, but there is no basis for assuming that such a one-sided advantage is the natural order of things. It is hard to dispute Moscow's view that the Soviet Union has as much right as the United States has to be a global naval power. Neither is it self-evident that the United States really needs to have the kind of unchallenged supremacy it previously enjoyed. As long as the United States retains enough military power applicable to the region to deter adventurous moves by the Soviets, security can be maintained.

Although the Soviets have undoubtedly narrowed the gap, Japanese and American military sources indicate that the United States is still ahead in overall naval and air capabilities applicable to east and Southeast Asia. If one looks not merely at numbers but at capabilities, some glaring Soviet weaknesses become evident. In a number of qualitative areas—for example, antisubmarine warfare capabilities (especially passive submarine tracking), on-board gear, communications, shiphandling, morale, and training—U.S. forces are believed to hold a pronounced edge. It is often asserted that with the deployment of the *Kiev*-class carrier *Minsk* to the Soviet Pacific fleet, the Soviets have made a major advance. But rarely is it pointed out that the *Minsk* is comparable at best to a U.S. ASW carrier, and it in no way approaches the capabilities found in U.S. attack carriers.

The ability to project military forces also depends heavily on a structure of bases, and the Soviets are far weaker than the United States in this regard. The principal base of the Soviet Pacific fleet, located at Vladivostok, leaves the Soviets vulnerable to being trapped in the Sea of Japan, since the four narrow straits through which exit to the Pacific is possible, can be mined or otherwise rendered unusable. Soviet forces have additional facilities far to the north in Petropavlovsk-Kamchatskiy and in Vietnam, but this does not begin to compare with the facilities available to the United States in Japan, the Philippines, Guam, and, under certain circumstances, possibly in Thailand or Singapore. Besides, Cam Ranh Bay is relatively easy to mine; it was not constructed with much thought given to the possibility that it might one day have to be defended from the sea.

Furthermore, a realistic comparison of forces must match not merely U.S. and Soviet forces but all those aligned with the United States—including Japan, China, South Korea, and the ASEAN countries—against Moscow and its allies, Vietnam and North Korea. This type of calculation makes the Soviets look even less menacing.

The Soviet Navy probably does have the capability to cut Western supply lines, but it is highly unlikely that Moscow would attempt such a move. The Soviets have been quite bold in situations where they could be confident that the United States would not respond, as in Afghanistan or

Angola; they have also been willing to support adventurous moves by their proxies. But they have always shown great caution in any situation in which there was a danger of a direct clash with the United States. Interdicting U.S. or Japanese sea lines of communication would be an unquestionable act of war, and there can be little doubt in Moscow that the United States would respond. And Moscow cannot safely assume that such a response would be limited to a local area in which the Soviets might hold a temporary tactical advantage.

A major study published by the Carnegie Endowment in mid-1981 concluded that the West's advantages in sea-based air power, ASW capabilities, and geography are likely to be central to the outcome of any naval conflict in the Pacific.[7] The report, reflecting the views of a panel of eminent experts, predicted that the West could gain control of the sea-lanes within a few weeks by bottling up Soviet forces in the Sea of Japan and conducting ASW operations against Soviet submarines that had been deployed in the Pacific Ocean prior to the onset of hostilities. Similarly, the report expressed confidence that U.S. naval forces in the Indian Ocean, with a significant advantage over the Soviets because of U.S. sea-based air power, would prevail, even though the Soviets might be able to inflict some initial damage on U.S. naval forces with a surprise attack.

Some observers allege that even though the United States and its allies retain enough military power to deter adventurous Soviet moves, there is a danger that the psychological impact of a much more visible Soviet fleet will give the Russians disproportionate political influence. In my view, the real danger lies in the possibility that alarmist statements about the psychological impact of a still inferior, if significantly expanded, Soviet Pacific fleet will become self-fulfilling prophecies. The more talk there is about the psychological impact of Soviet military expansion, the more likely it is that these psychological effects will materialize. It will better serve not only the truth but also U.S. interests in regional stability if we emphasize the facts that (1) the West retains naval superiority, despite the growth of the Soviet Pacific fleet and (2) an expanded Soviet naval presence does not automatically signify increased political influence.

The fact is that it is extraordinarily difficult for the Soviet Union to convert its military presence in east and Southeast Asia into political influence. On the contrary, the expansion of Soviet military capabilities in the region has stimulated heightened anti-Soviet feelings in Japan and elsewhere. Moscow's efforts to capitalize politically on its military prowess are further constrained by the weakness of the Soviet economy and by the fragmentary nature of Soviet relations with most east Asian countries; the Americans, Japanese, and Chinese possess a variety of channels through which they may exercise influence, but the Soviets, lacking highly developed economic and cultural relations with the countries of the region, do not.

Even where the Soviets have been successful in establishing their influence, they have found it costly to defend those positions. They were evicted from Egypt and Somalia. Vietnam is costing them between $1 and 2 billion a year in aid, and most Southeast Asians expect that eventually the Vietnamese will distance themselves from their Russian patrons.[8] Even Afghanistan, currently heralded as an example of Soviet capacity to act aggressively with impunity, may well prove to be a Pyrrhic victory. Although it can be predicted with confidence that the Soviets will pay whatever price is necessary to retain their position in Afghanistan, that price is almost certain to be a high one. It has already been suggested that Moscow's awareness of the difficulties faced by Soviet forces in Afghanistan may have been a factor in the USSR's caution about intervening in Poland. Afghanistan may suffer a tragic fate, but a cold calculation of the strategic significance of the Soviet invasion of Afghanistan could well lead to the conclusion that this "victory" will prove to be a drain on Soviet resources. In the end, the costs may well outweigh the benefits. Rather than making the Soviet Union a more dangerous threat, Moscow's invasion of Afghanistan may make the Soviet Union less dangerous because it may limit resources available for adventurous moves elsewhere. And, of course, it is always conceivable that the Soviets, having been burned in Afghanistan, may learn that such ventures are riskier than they seem.

In short, while the Soviets undoubtedly hold to their long-term goal of spreading their influence as far across the globe as possible, their capacity to exercise influence in east and Southeast Asia is likely to remain limited as long as U.S. and other forces retain their current capability to deter Soviet moves in the region.

In assessing the threat posed by Vietnam, one must distinguish between Indochina and the rest of Southeast Asia. There is no question that Hanoi will insist on dominating Kampuchea and Laos. There is considerable historical basis for the idea of Vietnamese hegemony over Indochina.[9] It was, after all, an Indochinese, not a purely Vietnamese, communist party that was formed in 1930 and played a large role in the struggle for independence from France. The Viet Minh fought against the French not only in their own country but in Cambodia and Laos as well. The victory of the Khmer Rouge and the Pathet Lao in the 1970s also owed much to the Vietnamese. The concept of an Indochina Federation is not merely a Vietnamese concoction; the French made such a proposal in the late 1940s. Demography and culture also suggest that Vietnamese hegemony may be unavoidable. Given the likelihood that there will be some sort of special relationship among the three Indochinese states, how can 50 million Vietnamese, generally described as more dynamic than the other Indochinese peoples, fail to dominate some 5 to 6 million Kampucheans and 2.5 million Laotians? At the very least, it should not be surprising that the Vietnamese are unwilling to tolerate a Kampuchea that appears to be a proxy for China.

Beyond Indochina, however, there is virtually no historical basis for any Vietnamese claim to hegemony, and, indeed, there is no evidence of a Vietnamese desire to dominate other Southeast Asian countries. The spillover of fighting into Thailand is clearly a result of Thai assistance to the Khmer Rouge, not of any Vietnamese desire to conquer Thailand. Ironically, the most dangerous aspect of the Vietnamese situation may be the fact that the refusal of the United States and its allies to deal with Vietnam increases Hanoi's dependence on the Soviet Union and enhances Soviet prospects for expanding their use of military facilities in Vietnam.

North Korea remains a threat to the south, and an outbreak of hostilities on the Korean peninsula could have devastating consequences for the security of the east Asian region. It would play havoc with the relationships on which the security of the region presently depends, and it would have deeply unsettling effects on Japan. The probability of a North Korean invasion seems remote, however. The North Korean threat must be viewed within the context of the growing ability of South Korea to repel any challenge from Pyongyang. Notwithstanding the setbacks of 1979-1980, South Korea's economic strength and growing military capability, together with a still credible U.S. commitment and an increasingly restraining Chinese hand, make it very unlikely that North Korea will wish to risk almost certain defeat by attacking the south.[10] The principal danger in Korea is that economic difficulties in the south, perhaps stimulated by another dramatic increase in the cost of energy, could produce political chaos, which might invite a North Korean invasion. But oil prices have temporarily stabilized. More important, most South Koreans are aware of the enormous risks that would ensue if political conflict in the south were allowed to reach the point where South Koreans had taken up arms against one another. They are very unlikely to let this happen.

Thus, a conceptual framework that focuses on the threat from the Soviet Union and subordinate challenges from Vietnam and North Korea seems out of tune with the real capabilities and, in some cases, with the probable aspirations of those countries. There is need for concern about the Soviets, Vietnamese, and North Koreans, but they are not the source of all problems in east and Southeast Asia. There are potentially serious problems that do threaten the stability of Southeast Asia, and these have almost nothing to do with the Soviets or the Vietnamese. These challenges are largely internal. Whether these threats to the position of existing governments in Southeast Asia jeopardize important U.S. interests is another question; in some cases, they do, and in other cases, they probably do not. But it is clearly a mistake to focus all attention on the Soviet threat, as if solving that problem would ensure the stability of the region.

Economic problems are the most pressing challenges to the security of many of the east and Southeast Asian countries. For example, South Koreans and Japanese view the availability and cost of energy as critical security issues. Significantly, a very senior Korean army general, one of President Chon Doo Hwan's closest colleagues, responded to a question about security I had posed in a July 1980 interview by asserting: "If you really want to do something for our security, persuade the oil companies to provide us with oil at lower prices." Rising energy costs, he said, were the greatest threat to the stability of South Korea. Emphasis on the Soviet threat and on the building of a united front to meet that threat may temporarily mask the fact that on key economic issues, the principal tensions are among the nations aligned against the Soviet Union, not between them and the USSR, with which there are significant possibilities for cooperation. For example, if the USSR lacks fuel, it will add pressure to world energy markets, while cooperation in the development of Siberian energy resources would ease the global energy situation and would specifically help countries such as Japan meet their energy needs.

If, as suggested earlier, the Soviet threat has been exaggerated and challenges to security are more diffuse, then it follows that the conceptual framework for U.S. policies should emphasize the strengthening of certain aspects of alliance relationships while allowing greater latitude to allies in other areas, should seek to establish a modus vivendi with the Soviet Union, and should work toward the establishment of multiple linkages, rather than a broad anti-Soviet united front. To illustrate the kinds of policies that would fit such a framework, I will consider specific policy questions concerning the way the United States should deal with Japan, Korea, China, and Southeast Asia.

Policy Alternatives

Japan

Without doubt, the U.S.-Japan alliance is the cornerstone of U.S. security policies in Asia. There is, however, considerable disagreement about the kind of policies that the United States should urge Japan to adopt in order to enhance mutual security. Those who consider the Soviet threat to be of overriding importance urge that Japan be pressed to accelerate its defense buildup. Some have proposed that Japan become involved in the defense of Korea, play a role in guarding sea lines of communication to the Persian

Gulf, and join in a loose anti-Soviet coalition with Washington and Beijing. The alternative approach, which follows from the conceptual framework outlined earlier, would be to encourage the Japanese to build up their defense forces only to the extent that they themselves see a need to do so. Washington should, however, urge the Japanese to make more substantial contributions to common economic needs and to develop a diversity of relationships with the Soviet Union (especially in the energy field), China, Vietnam, both Koreas, and the ASEAN countries.

What are the likely implications of an accelerated buildup of Japan's Self-Defense Forces? It is far from clear that an expanded Japanese defense effort would contribute much to the security of Japan or to the security and stability of the East Asian region as a whole. There is little doubt that the Japanese, by and large, do not share the Reagan administration's view of the Soviet threat. Although some concern about the Soviet buildup is voiced by certain segments of the Japanese leadership, numerous sources indicate that the predominant motivation for speeding the buildup is to satisfy the United States. U.S. officials report that they are frequently approached by Japanese seeking to ascertain the minimum defense effort Japan can make while still satisfying the U.S. government.

The Reagan administration is undoubtedly aware that too much pressure on Japan to accelerate its defense buildup may produce an anti-American backlash. In his confirmation hearings, Secretary of State Haig referred to that possibility, indicating his belief that any pressures should be exerted privately. The furor surrounding the use of the term *alliance* in the Reagan-Suzuki joint communiqué and the subsequent "Reischauer shock" (in which a former U.S. ambassador revealed the presence of nuclear-armed U.S. ships in Japanese ports) should remind us that defense issues are still capable of evoking a highly emotional reaction from forces opposed to the buildup of Japan's defense role.

To the extent that Japanese defense capabilities are being expanded at an accelerated rate in response to pressures from the United States rather than because the Japanese genuinely perceive a threat to their own security, it is being done for the wrong reasons. In the absence of any clear understanding among the Japanese of why these forces are needed, what role they will play in the defense of Japan, and what they can actually accomplish, it will be difficult to sustain public support for an accelerated military buildup.

The argument most frequently used to justify an accelerated defense buildup is that Japanese forces may, at some point, have to replace U.S. forces presently committed to the defense of Japan should American forces be redeployed to the Persian Gulf or the Indian Ocean. Although this argument has a certain surface plausibility, on further examination it runs into some difficulties. The fact of the matter is that the American forces that might be redeployed to the Persian Gulf are a carrier task force. It is impossible for the Japanese Self-Defense Forces to replace an American carrier task force because the Japanese have no aircraft carriers, and they are not presently planning to acquire any. If they were to develop an aircraft carrier, it would take seven or eight years to produce it, after another two or three years to work through the political process of deciding to do so. So for the entire decade of the 1980s, it is practically a physical impossibility for the Japanese to develop forces that would give them the capability that would be lost if an American carrier task force were moved.

If a carrier task force is essential to the security of northeast Asia, then the United States must keep one there. If a carrier is not really needed in the region, that fact should be clearly established. But it seems pointless to conduct discussions of the Japanese defense buildup as if Japanese forces could replace a U.S. carrier task force redeployed to the Persian Gulf.

The Japanese buildup being contemplated would consist of patrol aircraft for antisubmarine warfare, airborne early warning and command-and-control aircraft, and a certain number of fighters. Perhaps additional fighter aircraft can partially replace a carrier task force, but if fighters could do the job, then the United States presumably would have put more planes in Japan in the first place, rather than deploying naval forces to the area. F-15s based in Japan cannot strike Vladivostok without refueling, and the fighters Japan is acquiring will not possess in-flight refueling capabilities. Obviously, a carrier task force provides a set of capabilities not afforded by fighter aircraft alone. Thus, an accelerated Japanese buildup simply cannot replace the American forces that might be redeployed.

In any case, a modest buildup of Japanese forces of the sort being considered in 1981 is likely to be either too much or too little from the standpoint of Japan's defense needs. If the U.S. commitment to Japan is regarded as credible, then the Japanese forces are for the most part likely to replicate American forces; they may prove to be largely superfluous. If, on the other hand, as some commentators suggest, the U.S. commitment can no longer be relied on, then the Japanese forces presently contemplated through the end of the 1980s will be woefully inadequate. They will be far short of what the Japanese would need to defend themselves, if they were unable to count on the United States. So, either way, it is hard to see what purposes these forces will serve.

In addition, we need to remember that a Japanese defense buildup will not take place in a vacuum. If Japanese forces are built up at a significantly accelerated pace to the accompaniment of rhetoric about the need to confront a Soviet threat, one can safely assume that military planners in the Kremlin will view this as legitimization of an intensified buildup of Soviet forces in the region. If the Soviets feel themselves on the defensive, pressing Japan to participate in a tripartite anti-Soviet united front will simply exacerbate their feelings of vulnerability and stimulate further military buildup. Unless one assumes that the Soviets are already building up their forces in Asia at the maximum pace they can afford (and there is no clear evidence to support such an assumption), then it is safe to predict that an accelerated Japanese defense buildup will lead to further expansion of Soviet military forces in the region, so that the balance is unlikely to be altered in any significant degree. Nor is it likely that a Japanese buildup would save the American taxpayer any money, as is sometimes suggested. Once again, it is safe to predict that U.S. military planners will see Japanese forces as an essential supplement to American forces, not as a justification for reducing U.S. defense expenditures.

Finally, we may assume that the reaction of a number of other Asian countries to a growing Japanese defense system will not be particularly enthusiastic. The South Koreans should certainly be included among those who may be expected to react with concern to an intensified Japanese military buildup. Korean apprehension about the expansion of Japanese forces was apparent in a series of interviews I conducted in South Korea during the summer of 1980. In fact, when I asked how Koreans felt about the possibility of U.S. military assistance to the People's Republic of China, several stated they were less concerned about possible arms sales to China than about the Japanese defense buildup then being urged by the U.S. government. Even though the South Koreans fought a war against the Chinese in the 1950s, concern about Japan clearly runs much deeper. In Southeast Asia, similar concerns about a Japanese buildup have been expressed, especially by the Indonesians and the Filipinos. Some have indicated that their main concern about a possible withdrawal of U.S. forces from the region is that this may be taken as a pretext for a significantly expanded Japanese military presence. Although the concerns of Koreans and Southeast Asians about a Japanese military buildup may be outweighed by other considerations, at least they need to be taken into account when one assesses the implications of a Japanese expansion of defenses for stability in east and Southeast Asia.

To conclude, it is a mistake to push the Japanese to build up their defense capabilities at a rate faster than the Japanese themselves feel is necessary in light of the security threats they perceive. If the United States needs to keep a carrier task force in northeastern Asia, then it should be U.S. policy to do so, but it is foolish to imply that an accelerated Japanese defense buildup can replace a redeployed U.S. carrier task force.

On balance, the Japanese will be much better able to make a real contribution to the security and stability of the region in areas other than the military. Through economic and diplomatic measures, and through the contribution it might make to the solution of common energy problems, Japan can play a much more important security role. Japanese government expenditures on energy research and development are significantly below those of the United States. Given their perception of the importance of energy to their security, the Japanese ought to be able to develop a consensus that would support a massive commitment of resources to research and development of alternative energy sources. The United States might well press Tokyo to contribute large sums of money to such research, which benefits the Japanese and others, rather than insisting on a greater military contribution. In addition, we should remember that the Japanese view the USSR not only as a potential threat to their energy supply lines but also as a source of energy. Japanese participation in the development of Siberian energy resources might make a contribution to the expansion of energy supplies and to the establishment of a more balanced relationship with the Russians.

The security of east Asia requires not only military strength on the part of the United States and its allies but also economic vitality. Positive incentives—including economic carrots—must be offered to give potential adversary nations a greater stake in preserving a peaceful international order. If Japan's contributions to military strength are likely to be minimal, the Japanese can play a major role in the development of economic and diplomatic relations with the Soviet Union, Vietnam, and North Korea, as well as with China, South Korea, and the ASEAN countries. Rather than pressing for military contributions of uncertain purpose and questionable value, it will better serve U.S. interests if we look to the Japanese to make the kind of contributions they are best suited to make.

Korea

The choice with respect to U.S. Korea policy is as follows: Washington can make the tenure of its military forces in South Korea open-ended and refuse any contact with North Korea, or, following the conceptual framework described earlier, the United States can pursue a policy aimed at (1) strengthening South Korea in order to make it self-reliant, which would facilitate the gradual withdrawal of U.S. military forces, and (2) opening up contacts with North Korea.

The United States should strengthen its alliance relationship with South Korea by providing the military assistance needed to enhance South Korea's ability ultimately to provide for its own security. Rather than an open-ended commitment of U.S. military forces, the United States should provide as much military support to Seoul as is needed to maintain a stable balance between the two Koreas but not more than that. Maintaining U.S.

forces in South Korea beyond the time when they are really needed may in fact be psychologically damaging to the South Koreans since it suggests a dependency that does not really exist.

When the time comes to withdraw U.S. forces, it should be made clear that this is being undertaken neither as an abandonment of the Koreans nor as a punitive measure but as a vote of confidence in Seoul's ability to defend itself. Moreover, once U.S. forces have been withdrawn and South Korea continues to thrive, the North Koreans will no longer be able to contend that the Seoul government would collapse if American military support were withdrawn. The continued viability of South Korea after the departure of the Americans, together with Pyongyang's perception that Seoul's military power makes the costs of invasion unacceptably high, may even lead the North Koreans to accept the existence of the South Korean state and to begin moving toward some sort of modus vivendi with it.

The only viable long-term solution to the Korean problem lies in the gradual establishment of a security structure less dependent on U.S. military power on the peninsula. Although they may help to maintain stability in the short run, American forces cannot stay forever, and there will always be uncertainty about how the situation will change after they leave. A stability that is self-perpetuating, rather than artificial, must come from within—through the establishment of a modus vivendi between the two Koreas.

There is a strong case to be made for the initiation of contacts between the United States and North Korea, as well as between Tokyo and Pyongyang. If Pyongyang has economic and diplomatic ties with such countries as the United States and Japan, the North Koreans will acquire a greater stake in maintaining peace. When going to war means jeopardizing a host of beneficial economic relationships, Pyongyang is more likely to calculate that the costs of war are too high. Some may think it unrealistic to view such relationships as a basis for security. The real danger, however, is not that people will expect too much of these relationships but too little; an overemphasis on military commitments as the basis of security may prevent any real effort to test the deterrent potential of other means.

The Japanese are especially sensitive to the dangers of isolating North Korea. Economic and diplomatic ties would not only serve to draw Pyongyang out of its isolation, but they would also enable America to improve its knowledge of North Korea and develop better means of communicating with Pyongyang in a crisis. They might also enhance the development of economic relations that could help to stabilize North Korea's economy and make the country less dependent on Moscow and Beijing.

Although cross-recognition, in which the communist powers would establish relations with Seoul at the same time as the United States begins relations with Pyongyang, would be the preferred course, it is not necessarily wise for Washington to wait for Moscow and Beijing to act before taking this step. Moscow and Beijing may accord recognition to Seoul after Tokyo and Washington have taken the lead by establishing ties with Pyongyang, and after North Korea has had a chance to savor what is likely to prove, in the end, a rather empty propaganda victory. The Soviets already have fragmentary unofficial relations with South Korea. And as Beijing's relations with Washington and Tokyo develop further, it may find its relations with Pyongyang cooling to the point that some move toward Seoul might not be out of the question. In any case, one can question whether Pyongyang's propaganda victory would have any real effect on the Korean balance.

The central point here is that, even in the absence of reciprocity, steps toward the establishment of relations with North Korea need not be narrowly viewed as a concession to the Communists that must be balanced by some concession on their part. Economic and diplomatic ties with Pyongyang are useful in themselves for both sides. The promised benefits are not significantly diminished by the absence of reciprocal relationships between the communist powers and Seoul. Although the South Koreans would probably react with alarm to any U.S. move to deal with Pyongyang in the absence of Seoul's representatives, there is little justification for such concern. Even some South Koreans admit privately that they would derive a certain amount of benefit from U.S. or Japanese ties with Pyongyang. Most important, these relations, if developed to any significant extent, could serve in some measure as a restraining influence on Pyongyang. In any case, there is no reason to assume that U.S. or Japanese ties with Pyongyang would lead to any diminution in relations that they or other countries maintain with South Korea. No country is going to break relations with Seoul because it has established them with Pyongyang; Seoul's position is in no way analogous to that of Taipei. There is no danger that South Korea will find itself isolated. It is hard to see how the opening of contacts with North Korea would in any way weaken the South.

China

With respect to China, the United States is faced with a choice of whether to provide military assistance to Beijing as an explicitly anti-Soviet gesture and as a step toward a united front against Moscow or to limit assistance to China to economic aid and perhaps certain technologies applicable to military use. In my view, the latter course is preferable.

Any military assistance to China that is explicitly presented as an anti-Soviet move will needlessly provoke the Russians and the Vietnamese while doing little to enhance U.S. security. The Chinese have little money to pay for U.S. military equipment. Besides, their principal needs at this point relate to economic development, not direct military assistance. It is likely that China's principal motivation for seeking U.S. military aid has less to do with the concrete benefits expected from such aid than with the symbolic value of showing the Soviets that China has established a relationship based on military aid with the United States. How sending such a message would serve U.S. interests is difficult to see. It would severely complicate the task of building a new basis for cooperative relations with the Soviet Union, and it would tend to lock Washington into an anti-Soviet stance. Besides running the risk of provoking the Soviets, such a move would also trouble the Japanese, who attach importance to the establishment of a modus vivendi with the Soviet Union and who are also uneasy about the course that a militarily strengthened China might pursue a decade hence. Other countries in the region—particularly Indonesia—would also be very uncomfortable with a U.S. policy of arming China. It may be, in light of Secretary of State Haig's statements during his June 1981 visit to Beijing, that the United States is irrevocably committed to selling some arms to China. Officially, there has only been an agreement in principle to sell arms; as of July 1981, no decisions had yet been made concerning the sale of any specific weapons system. If the administration's course is already set, it should at least move with great restraint, taking care to consult fully with U.S. allies in Asia.

Southeast Asia

In Southeast Asia, the United States can pursue a strategy aimed at isolating Vietnam, providing substantial military assistance to Thailand, and maintaining the status quo with respect to U.S. bases in the Philippines. Alternatively, in keeping with the conceptual framework I have outlined, the United States could work to establish a relationship with Vietnam, exercise caution in providing military aid to Thailand as long as Bangkok provides support to the Khmer Rouge, and begin developing new arrangements to provide access to the military facilities in the Philippines on a basis that might be less offensive to Filipino sensitivities.

Isolation of Vietnam is, in my judgment, the most dangerous policy the United States can pursue in Southeast Asia.[11] It can only push Hanoi deeper into Moscow's embrace. U.S. interests will be much better served by a policy that gives the Vietnamese greater flexibility. There is no way that the United States and Japan can supplant the Soviet Union as Vietnam's economic backer, given the magnitude of Soviet aid, but it is possible to begin reducing Hanoi's dependence on Moscow. Allowing U.S. oil companies to operate in Vietnam and lifting the trade embargo would be important steps; even modest economic assistance would hold out the prospect of more substantial help later. It would, of course, be unrealistic to expect any dramatic change in Hanoi's relations with the Russians in the short run, especially if China remains a military threat to Vietnam. The Soviet Union is the only country that can offer Vietnam credible guarantees of military support against China. The establishment of a relationship between the United States and Vietnam could at least stabilize the situation, making it less likely that Moscow will be able to gain expanded military facilities in Vietnam.

It is, in my judgment, a mistake to allow Vietnam's intervention in Kampuchea to stand as an obstacle to the development of U.S. relations with Hanoi. Although no one can approve of Vietnam's use of force in Kampuchea, it is equally wrong to ignore the character of the government that the Hanoi-installed Heng Samrin government replaced. Realistically, opposition to Vietnamese control of Kampuchea in the present context is tantamount to supporting a restoration of Khmer Rouge rule. If it is morally troublesome to acquiesce in the use of military force to resolve disputes, it is perhaps even more troublesome to actively abet the restoration of the heinous Khmer Rouge regime. Clearly, the so-called third force under Son Sann has no significant military base, and it would merely serve as a front for a Khmer Rouge return to power. Opponents of the Vietnamese must recognize that there is simply no alternative to them, save the Khmer Rouge. It is also worth noting that living conditions in Kampuchea have improved substantially in the past year, to the point that conditions are now said to be better there than in Vietnam. It is quite likely that the people of Kampuchea are better off today, even under Vietnamese rule, than they were under the leadership of their compatriot Pol Pot.

The fundamental U.S. interests in regard to Vietnam lie in limiting Soviet access to military facilities in Vietnam and in encouraging Hanoi to live in peace with its noncommunist neighbors. Clearly, both of these objectives would be more easily attained if the United States normalized relations with Vietnam. Inasmuch as Vietnam accepted the previously enunciated U.S. terms for normalization in mid-1978, there is no obstacle, save the U.S. insistence on standing up for an independent—which means Khmer Rouge–controlled—Kampuchea. China and some, but not all, of the ASEAN countries might initially be dismayed at the abandonment of the previous insistence on a complete Vietnamese withdrawal from Kampuchea, but it is unwise for the United States to make its policies subject to a Chinese, or even a Thai, veto. Thai interests in a stable relationship with neighboring countries would be enhanced, not jeopardized, by the normalization of U.S. relations with Vietnam, even if it meant recognition of the Heng Samrin government in Phnom Penh and the retention of some Vietnamese troops in Kampuchea.

It is desirable to exercise caution in providing substantial military assistance to Thailand as long as Bangkok continues to provide assistance to the Khmer Rouge. Washington should actively discourage Thailand from playing such a role. If the Thai were not providing facilities to the Khmer Rouge, the latter would be significantly weakened, and the danger of Vietnamese incursions into Thai territory as a spillover of the fighting in Kampuchea would diminish. This would eliminate the principal reason for the increase in military aid to Thailand.

As for the Philippines, the United States should take note of the unstable situation in that country and the likelihood of future conflict with regard to the U.S. bases. It is time to begin searching for new arrangements that will provide the United States with the access it needs to military facilities in the Philippines on a basis that demonstrates greater regard for the nationalist sensitivities of the Filipinos. The best way to ensure long-run access to the facilities that the United States genuinely needs in the Philippines is to give up nonessential facilities and to develop arrangements that reduce the potential for conflict, rather than waiting for tensions to rise to an explosive level.

Conclusion

The fundamental principle guiding U.S. policies in east and Southeast Asia in the 1980s should be a balance between military strength and alliance relationships, on the one hand, and efforts to establish economic and political relationships with a wide diversity of nations, including potential adversaries, on the other. A multiple linkages approach may weaken alliances in certain respects, but it may also strengthen allies by giving them greater independence—for example, in the case of a South Korea better able to defend itself without U.S. forces or of a Philippines with the United States permitted access to military facilities that would be something less than full-fledged U.S. bases. In the long run, stronger, if more independent, U.S. allies are likely to be of greater benefit to U.S. interests. There is also need for greater boldness and imagination in exploring possible benefits of relations with potential adversary-nations. The failure of U.S.-Soviet détente in the 1970s, Vietnam's alliance with the Soviet Union and military intervention in Kampuchea, and North Korea's persistent recalcitrance have all been cited as evidence of the need for a more confrontational approach. The reality is that détente was misunderstood and relations with Vietnam and North Korea were never seriously attempted. Rather than sliding into a strategy aimed at building a coalition to confront an exaggerated Soviet threat, the United States needs a policy that shows balance and flexibility in dealing with both the dangers and opportunities of the 1980s.

Notes

1. This section draws heavily on Franklin B. Weinstein, "Asian Security in the 1980s: The Search for a Conceptual Framework," in *The Security of Northeast Asia in the 1980s: National Perspectives* (Working papers of the Northeast Asia–U.S. Forum's Strategic Issues Study Group, Stanford University, November 1980).

2. See Philip J. Farley, "U.S. Perspectives on Northeast Asian Security," in *The Security of Northeast Asia in the 1980s*.

3. John W. Lewis and Victor H. Li, "China's View of Its Security Position in Northeast Asia: Issues for the 1980s," in *The Security of Northeast Asia in the 1980s*.

4. Coit D. Blacker and Alexander Dallin, "The Soviet Union and Northeast Asia: Perceptions of Security in the 1980s," in *The Security of Northeast Asia in the 1980s*.

5. Richard Solomon, "Introduction," in Richard H. Solomon, ed., *Asian Security in the 1980s* (Cambridge, Mass.: Oelgeshlager, Gunn & Hain, 1980).

6. Elsewhere, I have described this approach as "multialignment." See Franklin B. Weinstein and John W. Lewis, "The Post-Vietnam Strategic Context in Asia," in Franklin B. Weinstein, ed. *U.S.-Japan Relations and the Security of East Asia: The Next Decade* (Boulder Colo.: Westview Press, 1978).

7. *Challenges for U.S. National Security, Assessing the Balance: Defense Spending and Conventional Forces, A Preliminary Report, Part II,* prepared by the staff of the Carnegie Panel on U.S. Security and the Future of Arms Control (New York: Carnegie Endowment for International Peace, 1981), pp. 131–37.

8. See Franklin B. Weinstein, "Soviet Influence in Southeast Asia," in U.S. Senate, Committee on Foreign Relations, *Perceptions: Relations Between the United States and the Soviet Union* (Washington, D.C.: U.S. Government Printing Office, January 1979).

9. See Gareth Porter, *Vietnam in Kampuchea: Aims and Options* (Washington, D.C.: Center for International Policy, May 1981).

10. See Franklin B. Weinstein and Fuji Kamiya, eds., *The Security of Korea: U.S. and Japanese Perspectives on the 1980s* (Boulder, Colo.: Westview Press, 1980).

11. For an earlier exposition of this point, see Franklin B. Weinstein, "U.S.-Vietnam Relations and the Security of South-East Asia," *Foreign Affairs* 56, no. 4 (July 1978): 842–56.

CONTRIBUTORS

ALBINSKI, HENRY S.: Professor of Political Science and Director of Australian Studies at The Pennsylvania State University. His most recent published books are *Australian External Policy Under Labor: Content, Process and the National Debate* (1977), and *The Australian-American Security Relationship: Regional and International Perspectives* (1982), both published by the University of Queensland Press, Australia.

ANDERSEN, WALTER K.: A political analyst for India and Indian Ocean Affairs at the Department of State and an adjunct faculty member at The American University in Washington, D.C. He has published extensively on Indian domestic politics and on south and southwest Asian international developments.

CLINE, RAY S.: Former Deputy Director for Intelligence (1962-1966) of the Central Intelligence Agency and Director of Intelligence and Research in the Department of State (1969-1973), is currently a Senior Associate at Georgetown University's Center for Strategic and International Studies and adjunct Professor in the School of Foreign Service at Georgetown University. He is the author of *World Power Trends and U.S. Foreign Policy for the 1980s* (Westview Press, 1980) and *The CIA Under Reagan, Bush, and Casey* (Acropolis Books, Ltd., 1981).

HELLMANN, DONALD C.: Chairman of the Department of Political Science at the University of Washington in Seattle, specializes in twentieth-century Japanese politics and east Asian international relations.

MYERS, RAMON H.: The curator-scholar of the East Asian Collection and a senior fellow at the Hoover Institution on War, Revolution and Peace, Stanford University.

ROSE, LEO E.: Lecturer in Political Science and Editor of the *Asian Survey* at the University of California, Berkeley. He has published widely on Indian foreign policy and South Asian international developments and is currently working on a study of India as a regional power and Indian and Pakistani decision making in the 1971 Bangladesh crisis.

SIMON, SHELDON W.: Professor of Political Science and Director of the Center for Asian Studies at Arizona State University. His research specialty deals with Asian comparative security policies in the twentieth century. His most recent book is *The ASEAN States and Regional Security* (Hoover Institution Press, 1982).

WEINSTEIN, FRANKLIN B.: President of Asia Consulting Associates, Inc., a research and consulting company based in San Francisco specializing in Asian affairs. He is the author of more than 30 books and articles on such matters as security problems in northeast and Southeast Asia, Indonesian foreign policy, Southeast Asian attitudes toward foreign capital, U.S. policies toward Asia, and problems of international competition in the semiconductor industry. He has been a fellow of the Hoover Institution and of the Council on Foreign Relations.

INDEX

Afghanistan: and Soviet Union, 18; Babrak Karmal regime, 26–27; and India, 33, 52–53

ANZUS: xxi–xxii; relationship among ANZUS states, 89–96 *passim;* contribution to Asian security, 105–10

ASEAN: ambivalence, 68–71; and United States, 69–70; military spending, 70; and China and Vietnam, 71

Asia: security concerns, xii–xix; importance for the United States, 75–79; and ANZUS, 102–5

Asian Pacific-basin states: economic development, xx, 12–13

Brezhnev, Leonid, 23, 46, 58
Brzezinski, Zbigniew, 5, 61

Cam Ranh Bay, 5, 66
Carter administration, 65

Carter, Jimmy, 3, 20; relations with Australia, 94. *See also* Carter administration

China: and Taiwan, 7–9; economy, 10; and India, 32–33, 43–44; and Southeast Asia, 63–64; domestic concerns and foreign policy, 121; and United States, 135–36

Da Nang, 5, 66
Deng Xiaoping, 3, 7–8, 11

Hua Guofeng, 7

India: strategic importance, xxi; rivalry with Pakistan, 25–26, 30–31; leaders' attitude toward nuclear weapons, 30; and China, 32–33, 43–44; and nonaligned countries, 41–42; treaty with USSR, 50

Indian Ocean: zone of peace, 44–47; and ANZUS, 103–4, 110

Japan: and United States, xv–xvi, 79–82, 129–33; domestic politics and foreign policy, 84; as focus of U.S. foreign policy toward Asia, 84–85; perceptions of Soviet Union, 120

Korea, Republic of: and United States, 77, 133–35

NATO, xi, 1, 19, 22, 87
Nayar, Baldev Raj, 38
New Zealand Labour Party, 101–2
Nuclear nonproliferation: 47–49. *See also under* India

Omura Jōji, 67

Pakistan: and India, xiii; and United States, 27–29; U.S. arms transfer to Pakistan, 53–56

Reagan administration, xv, 20, 115–16
Reagan, Ronald, 1, 4. *See also* Reagan administration

Southeast Asia: importance of, 62–65; maritime security pattern of, 72–73; U.S. policy toward, 124; relations with United States, 136–38
Soviet Union: security, xx; and

Soviet Union: (*continued*)
China, 4; military forces in Vietnam, 5, 66; military forces in southwest Asia, 18–19; and Persian Gulf, 21; and Vietnam, 67–68; and Japan, 86; and South Pacific, 107; national security concerns, 121–22; military forces in northeast Asia, 125; military forces in Afghanistan, 127

United States: foreign policy toward Asia, xix, xxii–xxv, 13–15; naval strength, xxi, 126; and Taiwan, xxiii; treaty with Japan, 2; military role in Indian Ocean and Persian Gulf, 34–35; policy toward southwest Asia, 36–37; and India, 42–43, 49–58; threats to security interests in Southeast Asia, 66–68; historical relations with Asia, 75–79; and ANZUS, 97–102; uncertainty about role in Asia, 114–18; foreign policy framework for 1980s, 122–29

Vietnam: hegemony over Indochina, 127–28

Yu Qiuli, 10

Zhou Enlai, 1